PENGUIN BOOKS

GOING TO MIAMI

David Rieff was born in Boston in 1952 and grew up in New York City. He attended Princeton University and is a senior editor at Farrar, Straus and Giroux and a Fellow of the New York Institute for the Humanities at New York University. His writing has appeared in *The New Yorker*, *Vanity Fair*, *The New Republic*, *Interview*, and other publications. With Sharon DeLano, he is the author of *Texas Boots*, and currently lives in New York City.

D0106610

GOING TO MIAMI

Exiles, Tourists, and Refugees
in the New America

BY
DAVID RIEFF

PENGUIN BOOKS

PENGUIN BOOKS
Published by the Penguin Group
Viking Penguin Inc., 40 West 23rd Street,
New York, New York 10010, U.S.A.
Penguin Books Ltd, 27 Wrights Lane,
London W8 5TZ, England
Penguin Books Australia Ltd, Ringwood,
Victoria, Australia
Penguin Books Canada Ltd, 2801 John Street,
Markham, Ontario, Canada L3R 1B4
Penguin Books (N.Z.) Ltd, 182–190 Wairau Road,
Auckland 10, New Zealand

Penguin Books Ltd, Registered Offices:
Harmondsworth, Middlesex, England

First published in the United States of America by
Little, Brown and Company, 1987
Reprinted by arrangement with Little, Brown and Company
Published in Penguin Books 1988

Portions of this book were first published, in slightly different form,
in *The New Yorker.*

Excerpt from *The Diaries of Evelyn Waugh*, edited by Michael Davie.
Copyright © 1976 by the Estate of Evelyn Waugh.
Reprinted by permission of Little, Brown and Company.

"Modern Times" from Nicanor Parra, *Antipoems: New and Selected.*
Copyright © 1985 by Nicanor Parra and David Unger.
Reprinted by permission of New Directions Publishing Corporation.

LIBRARY OF CONGRESS CATALOGING IN PUBLICATION DATA
Rieff, David.
Going to Miami.
1. Miami (Fla.)—Popular culture. 2. Miami (Fla.)—
Description. I. Title.
F319.M6R54 1988 975.9'381063 88 -2550
ISBN 0 14 01.1091 7

Printed in the United States of America by
R. R. Donnelley & Sons Company, Harrisonburg, Virginia
Set in Trump Mediaeval

For Sara Matthiessen and for Danilo Bardisa

"It was fun thirty-five years ago to travel far and in great discomfort to meet people whose entire conception and manner of expression was alien, now one has only to leave one's gates."

— Evelyn Waugh

Author's Note

A NUMBER OF PEOPLE in Miami agreed to talk to me only with the clear understanding that I would disguise their real names and stories. That seemed fair enough. Even when there were no melodramatic reasons for such a precaution, the fact remained that these people live in the city and I don't. Indeed, there are places in the book where the decision to conflate incidents was mine alone and stems either from the literary requirements of my text or a desire not to embarrass people who became my friends. This is a book of impressions, not a work of investigative journalism. What I have tried to convey is the spirit of Miami; I am not interested in, and have largely eschewed, the temptations of other kinds of discovery.

GOING
TO
MIAMI

URING MY VISITS to Miami, I often tried to remember when I had first started to think about the place. Though I was as a child obsessed with history, maps, and images of travel, I cannot recall lingering over any account of South Florida, or of tracing the path of U.S. 1 as it snakes through Dade County east of the Everglades. Surely, had I known that the Dade in question was Major Francis Dade — by all odds the most inglorious figure in American military history with the exception of General Custer — I would have been more intrigued. Major Dade had set out with his detachment from Fort Brooke on Tampa Bay toward Fort King, where the Seminoles had been ordered to sign away their lands. The Seminoles killed Dade and all but three of his troopers, the first shot of that sordid, merciless war of pacification which ended in the "Trail of Tears" and lasting dishonor for the United States.

Some of the Seminoles managed to hide in the fastness of the Everglades, but knowing nothing of Seminoles and having, then, no particular love of nature, the great beauty of that place awoke nothing in me, any more than did the dancing views of white sand and coral reefs. My dreams of the South hopped from some rather fevered fancies about the Old Confederacy straight over Central America to the grand, urban mathematics of the Incas, then back to the ravening gods of the Valley of Mexico. It was, of course, naive of me. We have our own ravening gods. But at the time, my peregrinations, both actual and imaginative, moved more along latitudinal lines, East to West, rather than North and South — very much as American foreign policy does today.

The one connection I do have with Miami comes from the fact that my mother spent a year on Miami Beach at the end of the nineteen-thirties. She was dispatched there, in what must have been one of the baroquer bits of medical malfeasance, with the idea that the sea air would cure her asthma. Perhaps my grandmother, like myself, mixed up her meridians. In any event, little lasting harm was done and my mother, her health patently worsened by the thick, equatorial air of Miami, was in due course removed to the less detrimental breezes of Tucson, Arizona. For her, Miami Beach conjures up hazy images of white stucco houses with pseudo-Moorish detailing and whites-only water fountains. This was Miami Beach before it became a retirement home for northern Jews, and, of course, long before the Cubans came in significant numbers to Dade County. My mother was six, Fidel Castro was thirteen.

The name *Miami* (which is said to derive from two Indian words, *maiha*, which means "very large," and *mih*, which means "it is so") was scarcely applicable to the city in those days. Greater Miami was still comparatively small, the city proper having about 110,000 people, Miami Beach with a permanent population of 6,500, and Coral Gables counting 6,000, though even then the area swelled enormously during the winter months. The expulsion of the Seminoles had not been followed by settlement, which dated, in real terms, from the decision of the great railroad magnate, Henry Morrison Flagler, to extend a spur of his East Coast Railway down to Miami from West Palm Beach in 1896. That same year, the newly incorporated city of Miami had just 1,500 residents.

Florida was settled from the north, and the first fortunes made there were in agriculture and its transportation. It was, in fact, the killing citrus frost hitting Central Florida in 1894 that tempted Flagler down to Miami. The story goes that while the oranges were dying on the vines south of Orlando, Julia Tuttle, who owned land along the Miami River, sent Flagler a bouquet of orange blossoms from the shore of Biscayne Bay. Miami Beach, whose tarred avenues seem fixed as the pyramids, was, before the turn of the century, a riot of palmetto, mangrove swamp, and muddy sand to within yards of the famous beach. It was developed first as a coconut plantation, then, with the arrival of the New Jersey horticulturalist John S. Collins, as an avocado grove. It was the failure of Collins's botanical venturings that turned him toward the mysteries of real estate.

By the turn of the century, Florida was already famous as a resort. Henry James went to Palm Beach in 1904 and seems to have been almost as mystified by it as he was by New York's Lower East Side. As his Pullman approached Palm Beach, James noted, more in puzzlement than in disapproval, "My companions removed, one after the other the articles of clothing that had consorted with our early start." Florida was a dream, the exemplification, for James, of the "hotel spirit." But though horrified, James was also clear-sighted. His hotel, he wrote, came near to producing the "illusion of romance as a highly modern, a most cleverly-constructed and smoothly administered great modern caravansery," all done in "the Moorish style."

Palm Beach was a Shaker commune compared to what would follow. In 1910, the Florida land boom started up in earnest. Collins, his avocados a bust, began clearing the mangrove swamps and developing Miami Beach. He undertook the great project of building a causeway bridge linking the beach with the city of Miami. The effort ruined him. In 1918, Collins was all but bought out by Carl G. Fisher, a self-made millionaire huckster from Indianapolis who had invented Prestolite. Fisher saw a great resort city rising along that fly-infested shoreline. He finished Collins's bridge, bought and reclaimed thousands of acres of swampland. Roads replaced thickets, hotels replaced mangroves; the bay bottom was dredged for sand to widen the beach. Fisher built parks, hotels, golf courses, and polo fields. Suddenly, people were as thick on the ground as the bougainvillea, the jasmine, and the sea lavender had been before.

Like the other developers who had seen the money there was to be made in South Florida, Fisher had in mind a kind of Palm Beach for the masses or, rather, a place in which everyone might think themselves at a place as exclusive as Palm Beach. To this end, all the apparatus of the fledgling advertising industry was brought into play (along with, on Fisher's part at least, a distinct reluctance to play host to any Jews). The developers did not wait for people to come to them, they went out and *sold* South Florida — sold it as a vision, a fantasy, a magic potion. The boom coincided with a medical fad for the health-giving properties of "actinic rays," otherwise known as sunlight.

The Miami Beach one visits today, despite both the improvements and the depredations of time, is still recognizable as the place those real estate hucksters fashioned out of swamp, grove, and bay bottom. All the clichés about the good life, the persistent harping on the fineness of the weather, the boosterism that makes Texas high school football look like a get-together at a Carthusian monastery, had their start in the South Florida of the nineteen-twenties. For the cocaine cowboys of today, sipping champagne in the private clubs and tasting rooms of Coconut Grove, the nineteen-thirties could provide no less a figure than Al Capone, the first of many mobsters to find Miami copacetic both for business and pleasure. Fisher had created two "residential" islands along the causeway, Palm and Hibiscus. Capone bought a house on Palm. Even the most recent arrivals to Miami, people for whom the name Flagler presents considerable elocutionary difficulties, know this. Haitian cabdrivers, fresh off the boat, will point the place out. Some even mention that the great Caruso — *ce grand chanteur,* one man called him — was brought to Miami specially to sing for Capone.

There is even, discreetly, Capone iconography. Recently, a cocaine ring in Miami was busted by the cops. The gang had been living in incredible ostentation, even by the Borgia-like standards of Dade County. They had dozens of cars, spent thousands each night on restaurants and girls, raced "cigarette" speedboats in Biscayne Bay, and didn't kill too many people. They were bound to be caught; they had none of the stoical patience of pros in for the long haul: it was all too flamboyant, too much like a movie. Indeed, it was as if these men weren't able to distinguish any longer between the lives they were living and a movie they were starring in.

The ringleader had been a national bicycle champion in Cuba, leaving during the Mariel boatlift of 1980. When the police (not the Basile-clothed glamour boys of TV's "Miami Vice," but the underpaid, outgunned husbands and fathers of the real Miami Vice Squad, whose annual budget is only slightly more than *one* episode of the TV series) raided his office, they found behind his desk a poster of Al Pacino in his role as the coke dealer in the film *Scarface*. When I told this story to a friend who knows the cocaine trade, he sighed. "In my day," he said, "we would have had a picture of a real guy. We would have had Al Capone."

Crime, looked at from a certain angle, is capitalism gone rococo. The real estate boom in the nineteen-twenties was certainly operatic in its unreality. Hearst's San Simeon would have fit in perfectly with the fake Spanish palaces the architect Addison Mizner was erecting in Palm Beach, Boca Raton, and Miami Beach. Mizner is a fascinating figure, almost the key to the whole period. Born in Benicia, California, in 1872, he was the son of the American Minister to the Five Nations of Central America during the Harrison administration. Addison Mizner liked to say that he had been educated at the University of Salamanca. In fact he spent all of three months as a student in Spain. In his youth, along with his brother Wilson, he prospected in the Klondike and traveled to Asia, returning eventually to his native San Francisco, where he became celebrated as a sportsman and a wit. In 1900, he published a book called *The Cynic's Calendar*, a compendium of defanged Ambrose Bierce–like proverbs such as "Where there's a will, there's a lawsuit." They seemed to sum up the age. In 1904, Mizner went to New York. By 1918, he was building houses in Florida.

Addison Mizner had always thought of himself as an architect, though whether he had actually ever qualified as one is open to question. Typically, when his credentials were reviewed by a Florida state licensing board, the examiners allowed Addison to skip the "technical" parts of the exam. But even if he didn't know how he did what he did, his talent is undeniable. Addison Mizner's buildings were described by Alva Johnston in his brilliant book about the Mizner brothers as "the Bastard-Spanish-Moorish-Romanesque-Gothic-Renaissance-Bull-Market-Damn-The-Expense style," and they were the perfect embodiment of that protean ostentation which marked the boom. It was crazy, it was ridiculous, but somehow everyone was taken in. Sort of like buying land in a swamp, that prototypical boom exercise in credulousness with a capital C lampooned only a few years later in the Marx Brothers' film about Florida, *The Coconuts*.

No dreams were too grandiose for the developers, for if they hadn't been grandiose everyone would have noticed that this wasn't the south of France or Andalusia, but a mangrove swamp one hundred forty miles from Cuba. Partly it was the shills who kept things going — Damon Runyon wrote advertising copy for South Florida land. But mostly it was just sheer, mad gall. In Boca Raton, which was meant to be the new Venice, Mizner dubbed the main road which led to his house "El Camino Real." Spain and Italy were always getting confused: it must have been those actinic rays. His brother Wilson actually proposed to the Boca Raton corporation that Venetian gondoliers be imported to ply the canal which ran alongside this royal road. Alva Johnston wrote tartly that if the Florida boom had gone on much longer than it did, there wouldn't have been a tile roof left anywhere in southern Spain.

The modern Florida of Epcot Center and Disney World is only the latest turn on the old Florida fantasy: everything is a theme park; every place is really someplace else, or can be if you want it to be badly enough. Consider the case of the city of Coral Gables. This was another Shangri-la built on the failure of an agricultural investment. In the eighteen-nineties, a minister from Gaines, New York, Solomon Merrick, abandoned his flock and came down to Miami to start up a citrus plantation. When it went bust, his son George came up with the idea of Coral Gables. The Merricks made $150,000,000 the first year.

Coral Gables was not going to be just a pleasant place to live, it was going to be great. It would have the best university in the country, preferably one specializing in Spanish culture. (This school was actually built: it is now called the University of Miami.) They say that George Merrick and his brother themselves chose the name of every street in Coral Gables. Like the Mizners, they went Spanish in a big way. Today, as one drives through the place, one sees this fantasy grown as rampant and exuberant as those varieties of equatorial flora that will flourish anywhere they gain a foothold. These men were absolutely stoned on the idea of Spain. Why not? Even Henry James, that prim, Anglophilic gent, actually wrote that as he approached Palm Beach he thought of "high old Spanish Dons and the passionate Creole beauties . . . of Isolina de Vargas, whose voluptuous form was lashed Mazeppa-like, at the climax of her fortunes, to the fiery mustang of the wilderness . . ." I don't know what it means, but it sounds commercial.

In Coral Gables, the streets are called Ponce de Leon, Alhambra, Cordoba, Almeria, Toledo, Alcazar, and on and on, mapping Iberia over again. The comedy of these decisions is that today they actually mean something. One is no longer talking about yet another Florida theme park, but rather of a city in which the majority of the people are Spanish-speaking. They know how to pronounce these names that have a significance wholly other than what was originally intended. I noticed this first when I saw that Anglos in Miami refer to "Ponce de Leon" as if talking about an English panderer, while Cubans pronounce each syllable with all conveyable delight, authentically.

The significance of these street names that identify Miami as a physical entity for the visitor, the resident, and the immigrant alike is profound. One drunken evening in Miami, Heberto Padilla, perhaps the finest Cuban poet of his generation, who now lives in exile in Miami, rhapsodized over the eerie predestination implicit in the street names of Coral Gables. "They did not expect," he said, as we weaved, our arms linked like parading bullfighters, through the mock Spanish castle-gate that guards and identifies the entrance to Coral Gables, "they did not expect the invasion of all of us, of we barbarian Spaniards. But we are here."

Suddenly it seemed that Miami, without having earned over time a tragic history, had had one grafted on itself by migration. The real connection to the past in South Florida ought to be with the Seminole Wars. Instead, developers came to a wild place, invented an image of Moorish Spain complete with all the modern conveniences only to find, fifty years later, that a real variant, a cutting from Moorish Spain, had in fact arrived. History had arrived aboard those refugee flights from Varadero Airport in Havana in the early nineteen-sixties. And unlike Los Angeles or the other great cities of the American Southwest in which, with every passing day, Mexican and Central American immigrants seem more and more to predominate, there was no organic connection to speak of between Miami and Hispanic America. For there was, first of all, no Miami. Beyond this, California, New Mexico, Arizona, Texas — these are the lost provinces of Mexico, never completely cut off from their Hispanic roots. But Miami? Miami was and is an invented vision, a fantasy of ideal living. It is, as Jackie Gleason called it, "the sun and fun capital of the world." In other words, it is a whim of its real estate developers. What was it doing now, I asked myself, caught up in this Spanish tragedy, this fiery node which now links the Americas? Which is the question that turned me South in the first place.

Americans remain ignorant or unconvinced. Miami remains the place you go to leave your troubles behind. On the plane flight down — it was my first trip to Miami — as I sat surrounded by loud, ebullient Spanish voices, I started to read an account of the release of the American hostages who had been held by the Shi'ite hijackers of TWA flight 847. When one hostage was asked about his captivity in Beirut, he replied, "I'd sure rather have been in Miami."

2

IF I was traveling to Miami to see new immigrants, there was, it seemed to me suddenly, a good case for staying home in New York.

The cabdriver was Ecuadoran. "Been in New York five years," he said, holding the steering wheel in what appeared to me — it was early in the morning and I was somewhat hung over — to be an obscure Inca grip of death.

As we proceeded, joltingly, toward LaGuardia Airport, I found myself wondering if all the cabdrivers in the United States were foreigners now. Certainly, a recent *New York Times* survey had concluded that fifty-one percent of that city's drivers did not speak English as a primary language. How surprised the well-Berlitzed European visitor must be when, mustering his stiff, serviceable English phrases at the taxi rank, he discovers the driver he has bearded usually speaks almost no English at all and has only the sketchiest idea of how to get into midtown Manhattan.

The Ecuadoran asked me where I was going. When I told him Miami, he laughed so hard that I thought either I had offended him or he was having a seizure.

"Oh, Miami," he said, subsiding, "I been there. It's Cubans, millions and millions and millions of Cubans. Not like here." Enchanted, I couldn't help asking him what "here" was like. He was definite: "New York, it's like America; Miami, it's something else. Must be all those Cubans."

It takes a man only a decade removed from the slums of Quito to find New York even remotely like America. I said this to him, though in a somewhat less offensive way. But he was having none of it. He just laughed, quietly this time, and repeated: "Oh yes, Miami it's something else." He was so entranced with this thought that we almost missed the turnoff for the airport.

All my trips to Miami began in roughly the same way. I would leave my apartment, find a cab, and go out to one of the three New York area airports. Out of the dozen or so trips I made, I encountered only three cabdrivers who were native-born Americans. One was black, the other two were white college students from other parts of the country.

After the Ecuadoran, there was a Haitian. He had a bottle of some particularly odious air-freshener sloshing noisily, a liquid seismograph registering every inadequacy of New York City's abraded highway system. The man said absolutely nothing and drove like a Shi'ite truck bomber. The third driver may have been a Shi'ite truck bomber for all I know. He kept up a nonstop argument in Arabic with his dispatcher over the two-way radio, changing lanes in the most perilous way imaginable by way, or so it seemed to me, of adding a vehicular exclamation point to his fervid assertions. It would have been an impressive performance even in rush-hour Teheran before the fall of the Shah.

The next driver was a Korean, amiable as a kitten. The problem was that he didn't have the faintest idea where Kennedy Airport was. I would have done better in downtown Seoul, though, of course, the roads are better marked there. The fifth driver was an Israeli, who puffed, groaned, sighed, and generally manifested his displeasure at having to take me out to the Newark Airport one otherwise potentially profitable rainy Tuesday in March. My excessive tip did nothing to mollify him, and he pulled away from the curb in front of Eastern Airlines Departures tires squealing with frustration. It was an anthology of Third World driving.

Andy Warhol said he liked airports better than other interiors because they were so clean, so neutral. I had quite the opposite experience. Perhaps airports have gotten grittier or, perhaps, even from afar, Miami had come so to dominate my imagination that I could graft its humid, bilingual excitements onto everything I looked at. Not that there wasn't enough play about the city in the press and on television to bend the perceptions of anyone who didn't live in a cloister. Mine was not the only mind in which Miami was ubiquitous.

At each of the three New York airports, my experiences were scarcely ones of Warholian antisepsis. Each presented, whether in the line in front of the ticket counter, in the milling crowd at the departure gate, and, of course, most noticeably on the flights themselves, different but intense hints of the Miami toward which I was traveling. It was a bit like reading reviews of a restaurant where one is about to have dinner, the way they do in France.

It wasn't that I was flying on different carriers: I took Eastern Airlines every time I went to Miami. Nor, I think, was it simply a question of my mood varying from travel day to travel day. Whatever happened to me in New York, I managed to put aside once I climbed into the back seat of a Yellow Cab, and, more and more ritualistically as time went on, peered toward the driver's hack license in order to ascertain the nationality *du jour*. I was invariably sober — scribbling away madly, in fact; everything resonated — though when you're on your way to Shangri-la you probably should smoke a little something. No, I am sure that each of the New York airports not only has its own distinct character, whatever one's destination, but that the flights to Miami have more of the stuff than they (which is to say I) could ever have used.

Kennedy Airport, which was the most expensive to get to, was far and away the blandest. My impression was that the bulk of the passengers on the Miami flights was made up of European tourists, cross-flying New York as they made their heliotropic way to South Florida, middle-class whites from Long Island who had chosen the airport because it was near their homes in Nassau and Suffolk counties, the occasional party of Hasidic Jews (they, in fact, were to be found at all three airports), and gaggles of amazingly fit young people, browned but as yet unwrinkled by the Florida sun. Occasionally, I would spot a Hispanic couple, and, like an ardent lepidopterist, spring toward them. The result was invariably disappointing; they seemed almost alarmingly respectable. Those perfect-bodied college students, in contrast, were simply alarming.

Most seemed indentured (a word they would have adored had they known what it meant) at the University of Miami. It was during my first flight from Kennedy, as I sat stuporously waiting for the announcement to board, that a tall black girl went rushing by me only to screech to a halt in front of a muscular-looking, blond-downed white boy who put down his copy of James Joyce's *Dubliners* with infinite relief as he rose to greet her.

"Hey Jeff, where you at?" I wanted him to say, "Page two."

Her every second word was *slick*. He didn't turn out to be a walking thesaurus either. The word he favored was *intense* — a tag he seemed to feel applied to any person or situation from his vacation, to his relations with his parents, to some dimly remembered party he and the girl had gone to together back in Miami before the term break. I was more and more convinced that the copy of Joyce was a bit of protective coloring the boy had assumed for the ride out to the airport with the family.

The plane was not entirely full, and so, as the stewardesses secured the doors, I gave in to temptation and edged into an empty seat directly across the aisle from them. The girl smiled sweetly at me, and, without being asked, helped me off with my jacket. I felt a hundred and four and that she was on some "Be Kind to the Unfit" kick. They started to talk about the University of Miami. It was extraordinary how much they disliked it. What were they doing in the place, anyway? What seemed to exercise them particularly, though these were very prosperous kids and clearly weren't paying a dime of their own tuitions, was the price.

The boy said, "The U. of M. is the worst school in

[17]

America. They charge thirteen thousand a year ... more than Dartmouth. They say they want to be an Ivy League school. They'll just wind up being a terrible school with Ivy League prices." He paused.

"Don't I know. But I told my mother I didn't want to go to an all-black school. I wouldn't go, I said."

Settling in to a companionate hyperbole, they went on to exchange hints about professors ("Oh, don't take that Myerson, he's hard" was representative), gossip about classmates, and somewhat rueful, surprisingly good-tempered accounts of their various curricular disasters. I didn't think she had a school of any color in her future. As for him, he would probably squeak by through "Business English," until, safely in retail, he could forget the whole thing. They had a collective moral age of about twelve, I thought unhappily, and a collective IQ barely above room temperature. In H. G. Wells's novel *The Time Machine*, the traveler discovers a postapocalyptic world divided between the perfectly formed, brainless Eloi and a hideous, competent tribe of subterraneans, the Morlocks. The Morlocks look after the Eloi, and, intermittently, pause to eat them — a perfectly sensible arrangement which the time traveler (played by Rod Taylor in the fifties film) screws up. These kids across from me, incapable of uttering a humane sentence, were Eloi. There was nothing whatsoever in their heads, and it was hard to imagine exactly where they stopped and their possessions began. And yet they were perfectly nice. I was terrified; I wanted to eat them.

The film for that flight was one of those late, decadent James Bond pictures — one of the ones in which Roger Moore plays Bond and looks, despite every effort of filters, lighting, and stuntmen, every millisecond of his fifty-plus. Throughout the first half of the movie, the girl attended to her nails, then, suddenly, she looked intently up at the screen. Moore was being bashed around fairly convincingly. It looked like a mugging.

She said, "I'd never go out with a guy who couldn't fight." This is precisely what Yvette Mimieux gives Rod Taylor to understand in *The Time Machine*, which is why, I suppose, he does what he does.

Worriedly, they watched Roger Moore slug it out. The boy's brow cleared. "Naw, it's OK," he said; "he's winning."

LaGuardia Airport, closer to Manhattan, was more down-market. Where the stewardesses at Kennedy rarely had any occasion to roll out their Spanish, their slightly more scuffed-looking colleagues at LaGuardia looked as if they got a lot of practice rolling their *r*'s. These flights not only never had an empty seat, but the passengers came aboard laden with enough gifts, car-seats for the toddlers, baby blankets, and outsized suitbags to make one worry seriously about takeoff weights. Bubbling up through the doggedly cheerful sounds of airline-speak, the greetings, the warnings, the reassurances, were solid clumps of Spanish. It was just what the Anglos said: Going to Miami was like going to a foreign country.

Many of the faces of the travelers were unfamiliar: broad, stoical, Indian faces; dark-skinned women with heavily piled, dyed blonde hair; a general increase in corpulence and diminution in height. Once, I literally slammed into a tiny, broad Dominican woman, who, receiving the blow impassively, simply turned and began to yell impatiently for her daughter, who was stuck, halfway up the aisle, unable to juggle both a baby and a boxed microwave oven past the obstacle of travelers shoving their belongings into the overhead racks. Later, the stewardesses, their lips pursed like Victorian aunts, would pass through the cabin telling people to remove their crates from overhead and put them underneath. All this took time. The air thickened. As it grew hotter, it felt, somehow, more alien. We were already in the Catholic South, not the Protestant North.

An example of this was the way in which people often did not repair to their assigned seats. Indeed, the phrase "this is not your seat" was one I came to associate with these flights out of LaGuardia. It was usually said through clenched teeth, every syllable distinct. Then would follow a rather melodramatic shrug of the shoulders and the Spanish translation. "*Ese no es su asiento.*" The effect was not electric. Lugubriously, the squatter would rise, moving back to his or her seat with a kind of sullen impassivity. It was always a relief to be airborne, though it was rare for a flight to take place in silence. There were too many kids.

Everywhere, the dramas of bilingualism and assimilation seemed to be playing themselves out. The *locus belli* was often the interaction between the generations. A girl in a white pinafore, a girl so washed and brushed that the word *curried* came involuntarily to mind, ruined one entire flight by yelling "I want my daddy," over and over again, with only a break for lunch, practically from takeoff in New York to the baggage area at Miami International. What was fascinating was that her mother and her aunt spoke to her in Spanish, and, indeed, spoke so little English they appeared not even to understand the offers of assistance made by one of the few monolingual stewardesses. But the daughter was doing her weeping in perfect English, and the mannerisms of her tantrum — its Americanness — would have been recognizable in Kansas. When, finally, the girl's mother lost patience with her and began to tease her by mimicking her plaint, the effect was ruined. The imitation was all wrong: it came out a thick, Hispanic "I wan' mí dadí," and the girl, if anything, seemed more puzzled than chastened.

It was rarely possible to sleep, to do anything, in fact, other than listen. The cabin pullulated with bustle of immigrant families, the scribble of traveling salesmen filling out their expense reports, of black soldiers furtively getting loaded, and the children of stern Central American mothers making faces at each other across the seat tops. There was no menace, nor was there a moment's respite. Travel was a drama. Invariably, one arrived in Miami drained and the Miami Airport is not a soothing place at the best of times.

Then, of course, there was Newark — my particular favorite. A friend of mine, a small-time coke dealer I had known in high school when he had been a small-time mescaline dealer, had warned me about Newark. "Don't fly out of there," he had said; "that's where all the dealers leave from." I hastened to Northern New Jersey.

Newark was never disappointing. Of the three airports, it gave the best value by far. The departure hall was invariably full of Latin men in leisure suits, dark-green, bottle-thick glasses, and cowboy boots. They carried monogrammed attaché cases the size of Homeric shields and seemed able, when they bellied up to the bar, to order their Scotch and water without actually opening their mouths. Certainly, part of this was a fantasy on my part, but, I am equally certain, it was not all hallucinatory.

The cowboy boots were a dead giveaway. In a room in the northeastern part of the United States, there shouldn't be more than a few pairs of cowboy boots. After all, the urban cowboy look crested long ago. But one of the easiest and safest ways to transport relatively small amounts of cocaine (a pound or less, that is) is to bag it in Ziploc containers and stick the white cylinders in the wide tops of a pair of Luchese boots. The metal detectors don't pick up either plastic or powder and the only way a dealer (these are midlevel distributors making their rounds) will get caught is if the police have been tipped off or if the carrier behaves like a fool. As for rip-offs (which are rare anyway in the cocaine business, where upper echelon dealers routinely travel unarmed), these are pretty much unheard-of. Another plus for the cowboy boot method of haulage, as well, since a thief would have to upend a dealer and rip his boot off, something which is hard to do discreetly.

I don't doubt that for every real cocaine dealer in Newark Airport, there were three guys who just looked like cocaine dealers. Certainly, by the time I started to fly out of Newark, the word in Miami was that the Feds had their eyes on the place. The air of menace persisted, however. Taking a Newark flight was like being in some Hollywood B-picture from the late nineteen-forties, one of those films like *Kiss of Death*, in which Richard Widmark seems always on the verge of appearing with a cup of battery acid in his hand.

Dark-eyed men would elbow past old women on their way to find their seats, and, once ensconced, their eyes would seem never to drift too far from those attaché cases whose metal-studded edges (a lovely, *West Side Story* touch) peeked out from under the seats. Attaché cases are X-rayed, so presumably if they were conveying anything illicit, it was cash and not dope.

The real interest of Newark was not the genuine dealers. Who knows if I ever saw one? Rather, what was fascinating was the way the Newark crowd seemed to dress like people in some illicit trade, almost as if the airport itself were a theatre. All of America seems more and more theatrical: everyone is posing as someone, and, with the Walkman, providing their own sound track. The fantasy counts for more and more. As for the truth about the three airports, for all I know, the Newark I observed may have vanished. It is entirely possible that the traffickers are all at Kennedy while, in Northern New Jersey, the people with boarding passes for the Miami flight are all relief workers, or nuns.

3

THE FANTASIES I entertained about the New York–area airports were, if anything, less developed than the fantasies Miami seemed to be entertaining about itself. They began in the gift shop at the airport, the first sight of Miami the visitor has after leaving the arrival hall. The entire center of the store was arranged almost as an altar to the TV show "Miami Vice." One would have thought that Don Johnson, the show's star, was God or, at least, the tutelary idol of the city. There he was grinning away on posters, T-shirts, coffee mugs, and brochures. There were also pictures of the black co-star, Philip Michael Thomas, and of the two men posed together. They were shown on speedboats, in front of their Ferrari, to a backdrop of the Miami city skyline — the perfect interracial couple, two male cops. Of course, the gift shop also sold all the sundries such places are supposed to offer, but one had to squeeze by the "Miami Vice" memorabilia to get to any of it. In no city, except, perhaps, the old Hollywood, has this ever been true.

Every city sells itself. A decade or so ago, in part

to counter all the bad publicity the town had been receiving, the city of New York came up with the slogan "I love New York." This logo, the *love* being signified by a heart, soon became ubiquitous on tourist merchandise and even official city brochures. Now, most cities have slogans, as if to say that they exist not because they are places where people live and work but rather as fantasies. The slogans are meant to entice visitors, drawn by such tags as "Virginia Is for Lovers" or the rather unfortunate "New Jersey Has Everything." You advertise a city the way you advertise any product.

Of course, resorts have always advertised themselves, and what is curious about the sloganeering that now goes on is the degree to which every state, city, and municipality tries to foster an image of itself as, precisely, a kind of resort, a fun house. Places like New York, which used to produce things people wanted to buy, now hire advertising agencies to come up with mendacious slogans about themselves for the benefit of the tourists. At one point New York was actually describing itself as "Fun City." But every city does it, and the airwaves are full of governors and celebrities shilling for their favorite locale. But Miami, I realized from the moment I stepped off the plane, was special. Nobody in the place itself had ever confused the pitch with the reality before. But Miami started as a resort; it has always dealt in illusion.

People like to dream about faraway places. It is conceivable, for example, that people in the rest of the country genuinely think that the Dallas portrayed on the TV show "Dallas" is like the real thing. But in Texas people just laugh. They know, for example, that Dallas is primarily a city of bankers, not oilmen.

The Ewings, in real life, would be far more likely to live in Houston, or, possibly, even in Amarillo or Midland. This doesn't mean that anyone in Dallas minds raking in a few tourist dollars off the Hollywood fantasy, just that, at the end of the day, they still know the difference.

It is so often said that the American Sunbelt is all the same — a homogenized, automobile-dependent sprawl stretching from Los Angeles to Houston and then from Atlanta to Miami — and that the real differences have gotten lost. America may all look the same on television, but it doesn't feel the same when one actually travels around; it only feels the same from the motel room. Nor are Americans, on the whole, quite as taken in by the TV images of themselves as they are cracked up to be. But Miami is a little different from the rest of America in this: its self-image has always been based on marketing, on the construction of new, improved realities. Miami invented itself, sold itself not once but several times, remade itself to please its customers. The restricted hotels of Carl Fisher gave way to the Jewish shtetl of South Beach, the Jewish shtetl to the Venezuelan tourist and the Cuban entrepreneur. As William Jennings Bryan said, back in Miami's infancy, "Miami is the only city in the world where you can tell a lie at breakfast that will come true by evening." Today this is done through network television. The Miami I had arrived in was once again in love with itself, but in love with itself as seen (the expression is from product advertising) on "Miami Vice."

The show was hot. Don Johnson was on the cover of every magazine in America. There wasn't a production company in Los Angeles that wasn't racing to imitate the show's graphics; trade papers carried long articles about the "cool" look of "Miami Vice" (the secret was no earth tones, one of the designers said). It didn't matter that this was a show whose premises made the film *Beverly Hills Cop* look as gritty and realistic as a Public Television documentary on inner-city police work; it mattered still less that the Miami portrayed on the show bore a startling resemblance to Melrose Avenue in L.A., or that the package was really little more than a rock and roll video with "tough" visuals. Everybody knew and nobody cared that a real Miami Vice Squad detective takes home about $450 a week, whereas each of Sonny Crockett's Italian sports jackets probably cost twice that much. All that did matter was that it was a great way to live. In real life (if the term still meant anything) the only way cops like Crockett and Tubbs could live in the style they are portrayed as enjoying is by being massively on the take. Even then they would still be in hock up to their eyeballs. In televisionland, if you open your eyes hard enough you can believe anything.

It had happened in stages. To begin with, there had been a series of events that had made the fantasy image of South Florida — the one summed up by the slogan "Miami the Magic City" — harder and harder to maintain even in a public relations release. The harsher realities were becoming inescapable, damaging both to the *amour propre* and the pocketbook. While Jackie Gleason was still golfing happily away on Key Biscayne, the city of Miami had grown into a place awash in black money from the drug business. This (and tourism from Latin America) was becoming the real underpinning of the economy, the heart of the city. The banks, happily turning a blind eye, made a fortune accepting drug money deposits. Soon the city was the point of arrival for most of the marijuana and cocaine coming into the United States from the South. It would have taken Pat Nixon not to notice. Everybody — the bankers, the merchants, the salesmen, down to the greenest bellhop straight off the boat from Nicaragua — was living off this cash. Everyone, as the heroin addicts say, was getting well. Even Anglo housewives from West Kendall were making $200,000 a year as realtors. One day everybody was happy; then, sometime in 1980, the shooting started.

The media had a field day. Reporting on a bunch of Colombian marijuana dealers peppering each other with Uzis and Mac-10s at every stoplight and across every shopping mall in Dade County was a lot more fun than a story about the SALT talks. Nor were these reports fabricated. Everyone who lived in Miami during this time had their own stories. Of watching the Latin family buy the house on the corner and then put in two million dollars' worth of surveillance equipment; of waking up to find a car with two dead men in it parked by the curb next to that house; of going into a changing room in a clothing store in Dadeland Plaza and finding a full clip of nine-millimeter ammunition stashed under the banquette; of being a newcomer in town and, while looking for a bank, stopping into one where there seemed to be no depositors except those Latin men in leisure suits, dark glasses, and oversized attaché cases. There was so much good copy, the national papers couldn't print it all.

Miami has always had an underside. It is said the

Mafia had a fair piece of Miami Beach while Meyer Lansky ran the Mob's Cuban operations in the nineteen-fifties from a base in Miami. Nor were the newspapers slow to point out other connections such as the link between drug money and the rise of Cuban-American political power in South Florida. There were dark suggestions about how these Cubans were connected to events eighteen years earlier at the Bay of Pigs and, perhaps, those of a year later at the Grassy Knoll. English-speaking Floridians felt that their city was being taken away from them and angrily voted down a measure that would have permitted bilingualism in city government. The bitter joke started to circulate: "Will the last American to leave South Florida please bring the flag?" And at a gas station halfway along the Palmetto Highway toward the West Coast, a sign proclaimed: "Now re-entering the United States."

Into this already hysterical, overheated time came what seemed like a cataclysmic event, the Mariel boatlift, which dumped well over 20,000 Cuban "career criminals" (as the police call them rather quaintly) on Miami, along with another 100,000 refugees whom the city was ill-equipped to provide for. Many had to be housed for weeks and even months, first in the Orange Bowl stadium and then in makeshift campsites. More shocking to local residents, who, whatever they thought of their Cuban neighbors, were at least consoled that they were white, was the fact that many of the refugees turned out to be black, or gay, or even both. Alongside these arrivals, there was the steadily increasing swell of forlorn Haitian illegals, and the decision was made in Washington to station a Coast Guard cutter in the Florida Straits to repel them. These shirtless negroes were actually landing smack-dab along some of the best beachfront property on the East Coast. No respecters of property, some also arrived indecorously drowned. A cartoon circulated of Lady Liberty reciting Emma Lazarus's verse with a slight emendation: "Give me your poor, your tired, your . . ." Then a beat: "hold the Haitians."

Miami was turning into a very peculiar vacation spot indeed, its troubles so compelling they became the material for novels like Russell Banks's *Continental Drift* and even a painting — Eric Fischl's brilliant treatment of grotesque, pink white holiday-makers baking under the Atlantic sun while dead blacks floated ashore like unexploded mines. There was worse to come. Miami was by this time being regularly described as the new Casablanca, which sounded rather terrific and Humphrey Bogarty, or as the new Dodge City or Chicago, which sounded slightly less terrific but was still fascinating, at least from afar. This new-found exoticism could be thrilling if rather disconcerting to older residents. Certainly they were not entirely pleased by reports such as the one filed by a German newspaperman in 1980. "In downtown Miami," he wrote, "a blue-eyed blond stands out like a European in an exotic land."

The city might well have borne all this had it not been for the forgotten group in the Miami polity, the blacks. On May 17, 1980, an all-white jury acquitted five white police officers in the beating death of a black insurance salesman, Arthur McDuffie. The ghettos of Liberty City and Overtown erupted. Before it was all over, eighteen people had been killed, including eight whites, who were dragged from their cars and beaten or burned to death. These images made

Miami seem suddenly leprous, the new Newark, the new Detroit. After all, who wants to spend their holiday in Watts? "Between Mariel and the Liberty City riot we were dead," said Stuart Bornstein, the owner of the Place St. Michel Hotel in Coral Gables, and even Miami's most fervent boosters do not deny that everyone was on the verge of panic.

(*Marielito* joke, still current as of this writing: A *marielito* is driving along on Interstate 95 when he gets a flat tire. He pulls over and starts to change it. A second *marielito* stops behind him, gets out, and asks: "What's up? Need any help?" The first guy starts to explain about the tire, but the second guy cuts him off. "No, you get the tire," he says; "I'll get the radio.")

But instead of dealing with the consequences of Mariel, or of the more intractable urgencies of black unrest, Miami caught its breath and kept pitching. The discovery was gradually dawning on people that these days there is no lasting bad publicity. Either attention spans are too short or a good huckster can make people forget. And what was bad publicity anyway? In the end, just publicity. Video had amplified Miami's problems, video would provide the way out. Liberty City was swept under the rug (as was another riot in 1982, which started when a Cuban-American policeman killed an unarmed black teenager in a video arcade), Mariel was made into a film starring Al Pacino.

Scarface was a surprise hit. While it was being made, it had been denounced by every responsible civic, church, and Hispanic leader in town. When it was released all their kids went to see it. Today, *Scarface* is a cult movie in Miami. I got a taste of this when, on Christmas Eve, 1985, I watched the two nephews of a Cuban-American friend — charming, innocuous middle-class boys — keep their whole hyperextended family in stitches while they performed their Al-Pacino-as-Cuban-coke-dealer impressions. Although these kids speak perfect, unaccented English (in fact, as I proved to them that night, I do a better "Spanglish" accent than they do), the two of them cavorted around their living room, stepping nimbly over the knee-high piles of gifts, past the tables groaning with food, and away from the outstretched arms of their grandmother, unable to stop pretending to be tough guys, to be *marielitos*. Posturing fiercely they repeated the film's most famous line, spoken by Al Pacino to his friend, who, fresh off the boat, is upset because an Anglo girl has turned him down: "First you get the money, then you get the power, then you get the women." Finally the two boys retreated to the couch to examine the home computer their uncle had given them.

Scarface was mean, realistic social commentary compared to what followed. "Miami Vice" was so cleaned up, so much not about drugs but about fancy consumer items, that it shouldn't have scared a soul. Instead, as with the Pacino film, the official response in Miami was, as usual, to panic. You would never know in a city where "Miami Vice" is now revered as an institution like the Seaquarium, the weather, or Jackie Gleason, that everyone in town was terrified of more bad publicity, of the prospect of still more Latin hoods firing off their heavy weapons in prime time. Apparently, there was even some considerable effort to prevent the show from coming to town at all. Fortunately for the city, it didn't work.

"Miami Vice" was a huge hit. More interestingly, fueled by all this caressing attention, this hipper version of celebrity, the city itself began to rebound. You couldn't, after all, buy the publicity that was garnered from that famous precredit montage of white beaches, swaying palms, swaying female behinds, jai alai players, the racetrack, the dog track, the boats racing in the bay, and the egrets rising from the Everglades. Since the show itself was, putting it charitably, post-verbal, the ensuing episodes did no harm at all to what are finally just a series of glorious images of blissful consumption all seen through a gauze filter and a Vaseline-smeared lens. The show was made by its clothes, the producers having uncorked a sartorial image everyone in America wanted to copy. Ironically, this "Miami Vice" look — theretofore unknown in a city that had largely gone in either for Cuban *guayaberas* or double-knit golfwear — was actually good, sound Milanese men's fashion refracted through the faultless taste of a clothing store called Madonna whose branches are in New York and Beverly Hills. But to the millions wearing pastel T-shirts and unconstructed linen jackets for the first time, this was the "Miami" look.

But what made the show's success so truly extraordinary, and differentiated it so radically from the renown of TV shows like "Dallas" or movies like *Saturday Night Fever*, was that it was sold not only to the rest of the country but to Miamians themselves. Nobody in Brooklyn really believed in John Travolta, even if people in Lawrence, Kansas, did. On a Friday night in Miami, everyone tunes in to "Miami Vice." The fantasts have been seduced by a final con, a con about themselves. They absolutely positively identify with what they see even if it didn't exist before it came on television.

Today, "Miami Vice" is the town fetish. People dress like Sonny Crockett, they talk like Sonny Crockett, hell, they are Sonny Crockett; or Tubbs; or Lieutenant Castillo. In other words, they are themselves, only better. Addison Mizner would have loved it. After all, the fantasy is not very different from the ones the shills put out during the boom, when brochures actually insisted that the entire Ivy League and one fourth of the country with it would soon pull up stakes and head for South Florida. Celebrities vied to get a piece of the boom, celebrities now vie to get on an episode of "Miami Vice." George Bush, the Vice President of the United States, was seriously considering making a cameo appearance; others, less powerful but more talented, have already done so.

Today in Miami, when people tell you that Philip Michael Thomas is about to open a club (some wags say he will start by showing a Philip Michael Thomas retrospective), they are excited by the idea. The prospect of meeting one of the stars of the show is held out like a priceless favor. Come back, one man said to me; I'll introduce you to the actor who plays Lieutenant Castillo. Later I realized that though my acquaintance knew his name he *preferred* to call him "the actor who plays Lieutenant Castillo." Their subjects didn't have such high expectations of medieval kings.

I didn't buy any "Miami Vice" memorabilia at the gift shop, but, before going down to claim my bags, I took a stroll around the airport. Miami as international city was a stronger motif than Miami as tourist attraction. The Chamber of Commerce is playing its Latin card. Why not? During the year in which I went back and forth between New York and Miami, the mayor and the county manager's jobs went to Cuban-Americans. Miami had buried its previous identities. Curiously, it was the first airport in North America where a good percentage of the service personnel — porters, waiters, and the like — were not black. No, it was Hispanics and Anglos, and no one else seemingly allowed.

As I walked aimlessly about, the predominant language seemed to be Spanish. Over the public address system, flight announcements were given bilingually more as is done in San Juan, Puerto Rico, than in even so international a city as New York or so Hispanic a place as Los Angeles. The decor, when it was not merely corporate prefab, was Spanish white and island pastel. "Miami Vice" again. A "Caribbean" boutique and a "Latin American" boutique nestled alongside each other. Halfway down the concourse there was a restaurant serving island delicacies — in reality, frozen conch, shrimp, and oysters in various gaudy arrangements. I bought the Spanish edition of the *Miami Herald* and its competitor, a ferocious right-wing paper called *El Diario de las Américas*. In New York, the headlines had been full of stories about Israel or the Soviet Union. In the Miami airport, those places seemed far away and Latin America, as a president of Ecuador had said, very near indeed.

By the newspaper stand, a couple in their sixties talked quietly in deep Southern accents, their bags making a little ziggurat around them. Shrinking against the wall of the kiosk was a small blonde girl, no more than eight, who watched with growing befuddlement the exotic-looking people who were going by while she listened, with the intensity of one who understands nothing, to the waves of Spanish that blasted along in their wake. She began to tug at her grandmother's sleeve.

"Grams, Grams, are we still in America?"

The couple exchanged a brief glance. It was clear that they themselves were feeling a bit lost. But they were game.

"Of course we are, honey."

There were shops that sold Florida oranges, pineapples, mangoes, and limes; others that sold exotic flowers. At a stand labeled "Café Cubano," I had the best cup of coffee I'd ever tasted in America outside the trendy parts of trendy cities. The girl behind the counter asked me where I was from, and did so in Spanish.

"¿De dónde eres?"

I said New York. She nodded, knowingly. It's on the escape route from the Caribbean.

Before going down to the baggage claim, I stopped in the men's room. A little brown boy, no more than nine, was systematically moving along the row of stalls, looking determinedly under each one. He asked me, in Spanish, whether I knew where his father was. I wondered where I was. No sooner did I lead him outside than we ran into his papá. Relieved, the man thanked me, in Spanish, of course. Later, a friend would tell me that Spanish-speaking people in Miami always assume anyone they talk to speaks Spanish. I didn't need to be convinced. As Frank Soler, the first editor of El Herald and now of a glossy magazine, Miami Mensual, is said to have remarked when the voters of Dade County rejected the bilingualism initiative: "Oh well, we'll just have to go back to using one language. Spanish, I mean."

[36]

But Miami, even in these first, disoriented moments, had other surprises in store. Down at the baggage carousels, it was bedlam. An undulating sea of brightly dressed people — impossible in the crush to tell Anglo from Cuban, tourist from local — jostled one another good-humoredly by the conveyor belts. My own bags nowhere to be seen, I stepped back from this free-for-all toward the relative quiet of the sliding doors. There, engrossed in conversation, stood a group of thin black men. I listened hard, like the little blonde girl, unable to understand a word they were saying. Was it some deep Florida accent, or, perhaps, were they Dominicans from the interior? I moved closer, affecting that air of reverent abstraction one assumes when one wants to eavesdrop. And of course, as I should have realized, the men were speaking neither black English nor Dominican Spanish, but Haitian patois. The French words began to penetrate my brain.

Every time I came to the Miami airport, these same Haitian cabdrivers were at the baggage claim. Amiable, if a bit aloof, they seemed equally puzzled by Cuban and Anglo alike. Again and again, I watched the confrontation between the blustering, well-fed locals and these refugees, most of whom were presumably in Florida illegally, from the poorest country in the Western Hemisphere. Anglo or Cuban — the difference blurred for me as time went on — travelers would approach one of these Haitian drivers and give him an address somewhere in Dade County. Almost unfailingly, the driver would puzzle over this geographical conundrum, clearly having not the faintest idea of where the house in question was. Then off they would go, through the sliding doors, to find or not find their destination. My own approach was to bluster at these drivers in what I imagined to be the tones of a French Colonial policeman. It didn't help their geography one bit, but did serve to establish a certain complicity between us. "We are foreigners together," one man said to me; we were lost in Miami, that mysterious habitat of the Anglo and the Cuban.

From the moment one steps through the sliding doors of the terminal building out into the real weather, one is enveloped by a different scent, a heavier, more redolent air: the tropics. That first night, the driver slung my bag into his trunk, and as he started the car and pointed toward Coral Gables, began to sing a Country and Western song in a heavy Creole accent.

4

I THINK I have always known Cubans. As a latchkey kid on the West Side of New York, I owed much of my security to the benign (and quite innocent) attentions of the two natty queens from next door, who used to appear almost magically and whisk me away to a Cuban restaurant on Amsterdam Avenue for those thick tropical milkshakes called *batidos*. As I slurped my *mamey*, papaya, or mango shake (I remember thinking, the first time I encountered good old American strawberry, that there had been some terrible mistake), one or the other of the men would feed dimes into the jukebox. They liked to play Nat "King" Cole's version of "Hit the Road, Jack," mouthing the words with flirtatious irony across the table at each other.

This was New York in the early nineteen-sixties. There were already many Puerto Rican neighborhoods in the city, but it still felt overwhelmingly Irish, Italian, and, in Manhattan at least, Jewish. Nobody except my Cuban friends even knew what a mango was. In fact, I suspect it was rare to find a New Yorker who knew what cappuccino was, outside of Little Italy or

Greenwich Village: New York before gentrification. The Cubans in New York in the late nineteen-fifties and early nineteen-sixties were artists, writers, translators, movie buffs. They included the playwright María Irene Fornés, the cinematographer Nestor Almendros, the poet Heberto Padilla, the cinephile Carlos Clarens, and the translator (esteemed by many as the most brilliant of the group) Ricardo Vigon. Many had come to New York to escape Batista. When Castro entered Havana, many went home. Few stayed, however.

I had less sense. By the mid-nineteen-sixties, my Cuba had become neither the island of my gay nannies nor the home of my mother's artist friends (rabid movie buffs, they congregated in obscure screening rooms like those of the Theodore Huff society, whose schedules have been pirated by every art theatre programmer ever since). The Cuba I had fallen for was a sterner place, its conviviality the hale, constructive fellowship of the scout troop or the kibbutz. In Che Guevara's words, they were creating the "New Man." That should have rung the alarm bells but it didn't. I stopped watching old James Whale films with Carlos Clarens (whose grandfather, Perucho Figueredo, had written the Cuban national anthem) and thrilled instead to the agitprop of the documentary filmmaker Santiago Álvarez. One is so new at sixteen that one wants, I suppose, to be even newer. In the winter of 1968, I went to Havana for the tenth anniversary celebration of the revolution.

A million people gathered that New Year's Eve to hear Fidel Castro speak in the Plaza of the Revolution. Even in the nightclubs like the Versailles or the Coppelia the floorshow would end in a kind of extravaganza of militarist fervor, however much it remained inspired by the choreography of Busby Berkeley. The chorus girls would stow their innuendos, square their comely shoulders, and, throwing out their awesome chests, bellow the words of the national anthem as they paraded back and forth across the stage. The audience, many of the *comandantes* among them, would rise, cheering wildly. It was a heady year for revolution everywhere, but nowhere more so than in Cuba in this, the Year of the Heroic Guerrilla. In extenuation, one can only say that the Vietnam War was every bit the obscenity we thought it was, and that we had, in effect, fallen for militarism with a human (even a sexy) face.

The year that was being ushered in was the one in which the Cuban government set a goal of a ten-million-ton sugar harvest. Later, this quota would prove absolutely impossible to fulfill within the set twelve months and so, in agriculture at least, the year 1969 lasted sixteen months. I would not, at the time, have looked kindly on such ironizing. On the contrary, I shamelessly aped everything my Cuban hosts ladled out. My enthusiasm was such that I managed somehow to erase from my memory all traces of my affectionate contacts with those "other" Cubans, the ones whom I was now pleased (having picked up this odious habit from my hosts in Havana) to call *gusanos*, worms.

Not that I had any concrete notion of this epithet applying to particular people whom I might know. I had long since lost touch with my Cuban acquaintances in New York, and those who had left Cuba loomed before me not as individual men and women but as a traitorous collectivity. I remember feeling slightly suspicious when, late one night, Heberto Padilla arrived at the Nacional Hotel to tell a group of us that all might not be as it seemed. It was hard to pay attention to these necessarily circumspect hints. And how exciting it was to career around the backroads in the province of Matanzas in the middle of a gorgeous florid night with a bunch of junior officers barely older than I. We shot off their .45s into the sea-blown air, drank rum and the imitation Coca-Cola Cuba was producing at the time, and, through the smoke of oversized Uppmanns, damned imperialism.

One of the instructive shocks upon reaching Miami was to smell that tropical air once again, the shock of feeling that distinctive Caribbean breeze against the skin, the sight, late at night, of the same constellations. My first evening in Coral Gables, under a picture-postcard perfect wafer of a moon, I was able to remember those days in Cuba more vividly than I had in the intervening fifteen years. At midnight, sipping coffee in the new Versailles (a restaurant in its Miami incarnation), as I listened to the speeded-up Spanish, the clink of dominoes, and reveled in the overwhelming smell of rice and beans, I could have been along Havana's Malecón, staring out toward Florida.

During this first visit to Miami, I was strangely uninterested in straying far from Little Havana or the other Cuban parts of town. Having rediscovered Cubans, they were for me in truth the only Miamians who had any reality. I was starting to behave as if I really had arrived in a foreign city. The same odd passivity overwhelmed me (a feeling which, in older towns, one overcomes by doggedly setting out to tour the historic sights) and, for a day, I stayed in my hotel in Coral Gables, listening to the Spanish-language radio stations, reading *El Herald*, undecided as to how I would proceed. Finally, I called a close friend in New York, a Cuban-American who runs a film distribution company with offices in both Miami and Manhattan. He was amused, unsurprised by my discomfiture, and came quickly to my aid, offering me the services of one of the people who worked for him in Miami as an interpreter *cum* driver. An appointment was fixed for the next morning, and, having overdosed myself to the point of eyestrain with late-night television, I went uneasily to bed.

I was up early the next morning, soothing my video hangover with cup after cup of *café con leche* from the Place St. Michel bar. Thus I was able to watch my Vergil arrive. José Arenal turned out to be a jovial man in his mid-fifties. He came bounding into the hotel, then stopped suddenly and looked around in some bewilderment. I would learn that he spoke almost no English at all and that the simple act of asking for me at the desk was an effort for him. I was getting ready to greet him myself when the clerk, who had recognized Arenal's difficulty instantly (and whom I had not suspected of being Hispanic), pointed toward me and said something in Spanish. The introduction accomplished, we set out toward Little Havana.

As you pull onto Eighth Street, a granite slab proclaims, "Welcome to Calle Ocho — Kiwanis of Little Havana." Our destination was the Pan-American Building, an undistinguished high-rise which squats like a prefab martello tower at the entrance to the Cuban business district. It is the home of both radio station WQBA and of the American Club, one of the most curious and emblematic institutions in Cuban Miami. The American Club was founded after the assassination of President McKinley by American businessmen resident in Havana. In the early nineteen-sixties, the club was re-formed by the leading Cuban businessmen of Miami. In the entry hall, Cuban and American flags flank a plaque that honors "the 25,000 political prisoners murdered by Fidel Castro."

One's first impression upon entering is of a blast of cool air, one's second of hot, loud noise. As is true almost everywhere in Cuban Miami, radio sounds played at high volume are inescapable. A Cuban newspaper editor, amused at my complaints about all these background effects, told me sympathetically that, the night before, he had been at an extremely grand dinner at the home of an influential Cuban family on Key Biscayne. The servants (Central American) had been in white jackets, the crystal had been impeccable, the Burgundy splendid, the meal a credit to the Italian chef who had prepared it. But from cocktails to the last round of brandies, the evening had taken place against a background of a Spanish-language radio talk show. "I only think it's odd now that you mention it," he said. "At the time everyone seemed to think it was normal."

Arenal took me in to lunch. Every table seemed occupied by groups of Spanish-speaking men. A woman in a severe Paul Stuart suit stood out like a boutonnière on a dinner jacket. I had forgotten how fast Cuban Spanish was, almost like Spanish jazzed by amphetamine. Nor was it easy to distinguish the words, which fall out of the speaker's mouth like Marines pouring out of a landing craft onto a hostile beach. The joke goes that in Puerto Rico, where Cubans run almost all the enterprises not controlled by mainland companies, the locals practice sounding like Cubans by trying to speak with their mouths full of marbles. "Imagine," said Danilo Bardisa, my film distributor friend who travels frequently in Central America and the Caribbean, "how Mexicans must feel the first time they hear a Cuban speak. It's like seeing overdrive for the first time on a gearshift; you say, hey, I didn't know a car could do this."

The American Club seemed to encapsulate all the contradictions of the life of the older generation of Miami Cubans. The club newsletter was still printed in English as well as Spanish, though a cursory look at the board of directors reveals not a single non-Hispanic name. Each newsletter contained a bit of club lore, which, invariably, referred back to the American Club as it had existed in Havana (or "Habana," as even the English version of the newsletter spelled it). Yet below such heartwarming entries as what fashion magazines used to be stocked in the ladies' reception room — the club was, and remains, unsurprisingly stag — came a menu and a list of future events few non-Cubans would recognize. Indeed, the menu was entirely Cuban, the week's specials ranging from *ropa vieja*, a kind of shredded beef, to *bacalao*, that is, codfish. Only London Broil was printed twice, once in the Spanish column, the second time in the English one. Bilingualism does, after all, have its little glitches. I mouthed "London Broil" silently as I imagined it might be pronounced in a Cuban accent, noting as I did so that the entertainment the American Club was pleased to present was "the famous Cuban humorist Tito Hernández."

"Home," wrote Lin Yutang, "is the food of childhood." Yet it was immediately clear that the American Club was far more than simply an ethnic enclave which had done a back flip on the way to Florida. This was nothing like the Italian, Puerto Rican, or (more comparably perhaps) Chinese social clubs one saw in New York. People didn't need to come here to reminisce about the old country; there were plenty of such places in Miami, my own particular favorite being the celebrated "Office in Exile of the City of Santiago." These were businessmen. More significantly, these were business lunches.

Most successful immigrant groups in the United States have begun their rise by doing business among themselves. Clearly, the success of Cubans in Miami was, to begin with at least, almost independent of that of the larger community. The first wave of immigrants (those who came to Miami in the first years after the revolution) founded the businesses that employed the second wave (those who came to Miami between the mid-sixties and the mid-seventies); in turn, both groups employ people from the third wave, though, of course, given the makeup of the *marielitos*, a polite way of saying given the fact so many are black, the process has worked less well this time around. But though the Cubans are famous throughout the Caribbean as clannish and as strivers, this alone could not account for their success in America, and more especially in Miami. After all, the Cubans of Union City, New Jersey, are not particularly successful and even a quick drive through the main streets of that town suggests something closer to Puerto Rican New York than to the Calle Ocho. It was the interaction of the Cuban migration and the city of Miami that produced the sleek, cocky prosperity of the men in whose club I had arrived under these somewhat false pretenses.

In New Jersey, Cuba is far away and Spanish Harlem across a bridge; in Miami, Cuba is with you everywhere. So is Latin America, and that was the real key to the Cuban success in Miami, and, to the extent that the two are separable, to the success of the city as a whole. It was Cuban-Americans who, more than any other group, seized on the increasing U.S. trade with Latin America — that essential economic shift which, sometime in the nineteen-sixties, saw the U.S. become far more interconnected with Latin America and Asia than it had ever been — to present themselves as middlemen. They spoke Spanish, the only time, perhaps, in the history of Hispanic immigration to the U.S. that this has been recognized as an advantage, and they were experienced in doing business with Latin Americans. Bankers in New York and Washington tended to be rather remote, not to say ignorant. As the Peruvian writer Mario Vargas Llosa said, only half jokingly, "They know all about our debt, but many of them seem to think Buenos Aires is the capital of Mexico."

In most parts of the United States, programs like bilingualism and what is rather picturesquely known as biculturalism are, largely, what in the New Left of the nineteen-sixties used to be called "cultural nationalism." Whether the Chicano militants in California and Texas know it or not, their version will abut, by the beginning of the next century, what will probably be a very messy, Quebec-style autonomist political movement. Already Chicano intellectuals talk about a nation called *Azatlán*. If a country like Belgium cannot escape the rigors of bilingualism, why should a country like California? But in Miami, all these questions, like so many others, have been turned on their ear.

The crossed flags of Cuba and the United States

that stood at the threshold of the American Club were simply accurate iconic representations of the reality of Miami. These businessmen, and their more assimilated brethren as well, had not let go of Cuba even as they were declaring themselves fiercely, possessively American. That was why it was right that they had taken the name of the club with them as they left Havana for the last time. Nor was their attitude at all generational. Miami is full of glossy magazines and newspapers that are printed either exclusively in Spanish or bilingually. The best of them is probably *Miami Mensual* (Miami Monthly), edited by Frank Soler. Recently, the magazine ran a spirited piece by a young Cuban-American woman named Arely Ruiz. It is a classic statement of the way Cuban Miami wants to understand its Cuban and its American nature. The world, according to Ms. Ruiz, was growing smaller, more multicultural. Coming out from the shade of Marshall McLuhan, she went on to argue that no one needed to give up their roots, that there was no contradiction between being a Cuban and being an American. All of this was presented with credible passion and with fervent patriotism. "The flag," Ms. Ruiz concluded, pointedly answering all those Anglo jokes, "stays here."

The world of Arely Ruiz, or even of Frank Soler, is of course far more Americanized than that of most people at the American Club. What marked everyone was the will to succeed. "When I got to Miami," Frank Soler told me, "I had never worked a day in my life. I went from having money to unloading garbage at the back of a food market." But there he was, the image of success, talking urbanely in his office in Coral Gables. And here were the members of the

American Club, hatching not exile plots but rather business deals. Surely most of them had been equally penniless when they had arrived in Florida, but now it was mostly silk ties and platinum watches. They were a raging success, just like their city — the one that I could discern through the gleaming plate glass, first as a shapeless expanse of low-slung houses, until, miles away, the skyline of the center city rose jaggedly and, beyond it, the glinting waters of Biscayne Bay.

After we had finished our *vaca frita* and our *escabeche* and had regained our equilibrium with dosings of Cuban coffee, Arenal led me downstairs to WQBA. Suspecting that he was combining some chore of his own with his efforts on my behalf, I had not been looking forward to our visit. In fact, I was to return repeatedly, mesmerized by the floating crap game of middle-aged men kibitzing outside the broadcast studios, the purposeful young members of the station staff striding to and fro, switching effortlessly from Spanish to English (English even in the Calle Ocho radio station!) and back again, and, equally enthralling, the overcrowded booty of mementos lying in glass boxes along the walls — certificates of public service, testimonials proclaiming successive rises in market share, testimonials proclaiming various accruals of honor, and, dominating the rest, dozens of images of Cuba and of the national hero, José Martí.

Martí is perhaps the only great revolutionary figure claimed by both communists and their opponents. Indeed it is one of the odder details of the Cuban diaspora that parks and monuments in Miami often bear the same names as similar parks and monuments in Havana and Santiago de Cuba. Thus one can play baseball (the most popular sport, it need hardly be added, in Cuba as well as in the United States) in front of a heroic statue of Antonio Maceo (the black general who was one of the heroes of Cuba's struggle for independence from Spain) in Miami and in Havana. The images of Martí, though, while common in Cuba, are ubiquitous in Miami. They, along with images of the island itself, make up much of the city's civic art despite recent attempts to adorn at least the Metrorail system with the more advanced creations of modernism. Whether they are formed out of steel at the entrance to a park or simply daubed heartily if inexpertly on the wall of a playground or sold for display in offices and homes, these icons provide another message, more nuanced, perhaps, than the cheery biculturalism of the Chamber of Commerce. They say: "This is a Cuban town. Don't let the rest fool you." These were not the kinds of meaningless sculptures one sees in most American cities, those forlorn bronze references to the Civil War or some statesman from the Gilded Age. These monuments still exude a living aura, the kind of power monuments used to exude before they were superseded, in the public spaces of America, by the incomprehensible geometry of abstract sculpture.

Less fixed than the public memorials to Cuba were the physical types of the Miami Cubans themselves. To an outsider, the physical differences between older Cuban men and women and their American-born, or, at least, American-raised offspring is absolutely remarkable. The older Cubans I saw at WQBA were for the most part short and thickly constructed. Clad in their tight-fitting *guayaberas* (unlike Anglos who affect the style, Cuban men don't seem to mind letting their paunches show), drinking their endless cups of coffee, and punctuating their voluble sentences with baroque, flamboyant, almost caricatural gestures, they seemed absolutely foreign, epidermally unmarked by the lives they had made in America. Arenal was very much of this type, and seemed rather ill at ease with Cuban-Americans of his children's generation. I was not surprised. Young Cuban men looked very much like other Americans. Since they are, overwhelmingly, white, it is quite easy to mistake a young Cuban couple sitting in one of the all-night cafés of Little Havana for a couple of Anglo tourists.

In a sense, they are. Rarely did I see anyone young who was monolingual in Spanish. The norm was a kind of mysteriously arrived-at diglossia. One would hear a group of people speaking accentless Sunbelt American suddenly shift, apparently on pure whim (though a linguist could doubtless pick up the clues), to the swift staccato of Cuban Spanish. The younger children seemed often to be monolingual in English. It was difficult, I noticed with some surprise, for Roberto Fabricio, then the editor of *El Herald*, to get his kids to speak Spanish to anyone younger than their grandmother. They are not, I suspect, atypical for all the brave talk about biculturalism. In a city as television-obsessed as Miami, the blandishments of English are powerful. The Spanish soaps on SIN are no match for the techno-glitz of Burbank. Arenal's own sons, born in Cuba but raised in Miami, were cases in point. Largely, they spoke English to each other, a linguistic defection Arenal accepted with characteristic decency. What concerned him more was that his sons did not seem very interested in reading. "I don't care in which language they do it," he said a bit hopelessly, "just so they read something." But, alas, biculturalism in Miami is big on the "bi" and not so hot on the "culture" except in the simplest, ethnic denotation.

Not that Miami is any more barbarous than the rest of the country. Quite the reverse. The older Cubans have a vestigial respect for art much like that the first generation of European immigrants had at the turn of the century. But in the brilliant sunshine of Florida, books look odd, almost out of place. These tall, rangy Cuban men radiated a very American, very postliterate kind of self-confidence — an effortless physicality which is often called "Texan." This corporeal transformation is something that is often remarked on by the people who have taught in Miami's high schools and universities over the last decade and a half. Where, fifteen years ago, Cuban girls usually had the big bottoms and generous figures of their mothers, they are now as lithe — and sometimes as anorectic — as their Anglo sisters. Dahlia Morgan, who directs the art gallery at Florida International University, told me that when she proposed a Cuban lunch to one of her (Cuban-American) assistants, the girl agreed happily but noted that she permitted herself the fattening indulgence of rice and beans — "Christians and Moors," as Cubans sometimes call them — only a few times a year.

Within hours of plunging into the reality of Cuban Miami, I had found it familiar, foreign, unique, alien, and, increasingly familiar again. It wasn't, of course, that I had suddenly become persuaded that this was another immigrant town, like Cleveland, say, in which the patterns of the Germans, the Poles, or the Jews would be reproduced. There was no need to see Miami in order to understand that the Spanish language was in North America to stay. The inevitability of this should be clear if one tries to imagine what would have happened had it been Italy, not Mexico, which rested on the other side of the Rio Grande. To put the matter gently, a great many Italian-Americans would still speak Italian, and many, no doubt, would speak no English at all.

I was accustomed to the Hispanicized downtowns of cities like Los Angeles, where one can blink for a moment, then open one's eyes and believe oneself in some new, mestizo nation, or, perhaps, in a colony of the United States. In Miami, the image of Havana — which is never too far off for a visitor with eyes to see — was so mesmerizing that it left me ready to welcome every evidence of the foreign but unprepared for the degree of assimilation. For whether the scene was that of Cuban-American teenagers joyriding ritualistically through Coconut Grove on Saturday nights, heavy metal rock blaring through their car speakers, or the sight of the largely Cuban crowd in the Orange Bowl cheering on the football Hurricanes of the University of Miami, the young people, at least, seemed thoroughly at home — their vices and virtues already American to the core.

5

AT STATION WQBA, "La Cubanísima," the morning disc jockey is running a quiz about the geography of old Havana. "What," he asks, his shoulders swaying to the tune he has just segued out, "was the name of the most upright street in Havana?" After a suitable pause, he supplies the answer: "Virtudes." Virtues Street. Outside the glass booth, groups of *guayabera*-clad men loiter contentedly, drinking little cups of thick espresso from paper containers. The view of Miami from the huge windows is glorious. When the speakers in this waiting area blare out the deejay's question, the men convulse with laughter. "I can tell you the name of the least virtuous street in Havana," one of them calls out. The jock waves at them, as if he has heard. Turning back to the microphone, he adds that the communists have probably changed all the old street names anyway. Then he shoves in a cassette, the music fills the hall, and I see the man half-rising from his seat to dance along to the salsa beat that goes on twenty-four hours a day on this, the "Cubanest" radio station in America's "Cubanest" town.

WQBA is largely a music station, and, as such, relatively less occupied with politics than others on the Calle Ocho. Even today, however, the ideological wars rage unabated on the AM airwaves. I was haunted by those radio stations, by the fanatic pronouncements of Cuban talk-show hosts, the murderous political arguments (all on the right, of course), the raw, stereotypical anticommunism. This seemed like the Miami people outside the city talked about, the last Batistiano·town in Cuba, the rear echelon of the Nicaraguan *contras*, the place of exile (and possibly of business) of every fascist thug in the Americas. To be sure, there were moderating voices. Heberto Padilla, for example, for a time did a regular broadcast for *La Cadena Azúl* in which he tried to inject, as someone who had left Cuba in 1981, a little realism into the debate. He was not in the majority.

My obsession was partly a pure question of decibels. In a city where everyone drives, the radio assumes a more intimate, essential role than it occupies in places where it serves as little more than a wake-up call or distant background noise. Moreover, the volume at which Cubans seemed to play their radios (sometimes simultaneously with their televisions, a psychosis-inducing mixture) was itself a kind of falsifying enhancer of the importance of the Calle Ocho stations. Often in Miami, I would get into someone's car to find, as he started the engine, that I was being bombarded by an almost life-threatening barrage of sound. It was like having one of the dictators from a Latin American novel screaming in your ear.

Opinion was mixed as to the importance of these stations. Some thought they were dying out. A friend told of a conversation with one of the owners of a

Calle station during which the man had sighed regretfully and remarked, "Every time I read the obituary column, I feel I've lost three of my listeners." This is very much the view which insists that Spanish will decline in importance over time. Those who subscribe to it are also given to reminding visitors that such newspapers as the *St. Louis Post-Dispatch* started as German-language papers and that the Texas Declaration of Independence was proclaimed in English, Spanish, and German. By the same token, or so the argument runs, the political fanaticism of the broadcasts is little more than a certain ferocious nostalgia, like an old dog too lame and sick to know he is lame and sick.

There must be some truth to this view. Certainly the geriatric contingent among listeners is high. Understandably, the older people simply cannot reconcile themselves to the idea that they will never return to Cuba. One day, walking in Little Havana, I heard a fierce croaking, like a nest of rabid bullfrogs. Eventually I was able to sort out human speech patterns. One voice thundered: "We will return to our homeland." Another chimed in: "The Cuban will rise up." And a third: "And we will hang Castro by his heels." I turned to face three ancient geezers, parked sedately in front of a domino board. They would, I mused, have enough on their hands making it across the parking lot back to their porches, never mind liberating Oriente.

Moreover, the level of actual violence, as opposed to verbal hyperbole, was, by all accounts, sharply reduced from what it had been in earlier years. All the gunmen, not just these domino players, were getting a little long in the tooth. Some of the most fearsome of them had been killed in drug wars, private vendettas, or in vain attempts to foment trouble on the island. Many had declared themselves in retirement. "No one's been blown away here in years," said a young Cuban entrepreneur whose brother had served in Brigade 2506 at the Bay of Pigs. A surer indicator seemed to me the fact that at the annual Cuban parade there had been only one overtly political float. All the others had carried beauty queens, festive evocations of Cuba, displays of U.S. and regional patriotism, and advertisements. Banal perhaps, but a step in the right direction.

But leaving aside the question of whether, in fact, Miami was going to become another Boston, and the Cubans under their new mayor Xavier Suárez like the Irish in the days of Mayor Curley, I was by no means so sure that the political situation had been as transformed as all that. Stations folded, but others arose to take their place. Recently, a well-known South Florida "easy listening" station had sold its 50,000 watt transmitter to the newly established Radio Mambí. Not only was it clear that the English-language station no longer could attract an audience sufficient to justify such a powerful transmitter, it was apparent that the crowded field of Spanish-language broadcasting in Miami had room for one more.

Radio Mambí was set up as a political organ. The Mambises were guerrilla fighters who fought the Spaniards to a standstill during the Cuban Wars of Independence. One of the avowed purposes of acquiring such a powerful signal was to enable the station's broadcasts to reach Cuba itself. Indeed, the full-page ads that ran in the Spanish-language press to announce Mambí featured a map of the Caribbean in which a signal from Miami was shown enveloping Cuba. Mambí was a second choice as a name. The station's backers had, at first, wanted to use "Radio Martí," but this had been preempted by the decision of the Voice of America to use the name for its own service directed at Cuba. Nonetheless, during the first days of Mambí's operation, the announcers kept slipping. Every time they had to identify their station one could hear them hesitate. At times, one would even hear: "*Aquí, radio Mar . . . Mambí.*" Only on a Spanish-language station in Miami does the concept *stentorian indecision* have any meaning.

Patiently, Arenal took me around to each of these stations. At WRHC, Thomas Regalado, Jr., then the news director (his father also worked at the station, after having spent over twenty years as a political prisoner in Cuba), had a decal over his desk of crossed American and Cuban flags under the legend "Libertad vs. Communismo: Reagan-Bush '84." This was late 1985 and the Reagan-Bush election stickers were everywhere, almost as common to behold as images of Martí or Don Johnson. It was as if, somehow, the Republicans had lost rather than won — neoconservatism's answer to the pathetic fallacy. Or, perhaps, these stickers were declarations of loyalty, like the St. Christopher medals that used to grace Catholic dashboards all over America until the revisionists of Vatican II struck the saint from the calendar.

Over lunch at the Centro Vasco restaurant, which boasted in its foyer a signed photo of President Reagan, Arenal told me gleefully how, the night before the election, the President had come to Little Havana. The crowds had been waiting all day, and Florida, it need hardly be recalled, is hardly a place where it is comfortable to wait in the sun. Nevertheless, while the reporters scribbled and the sheriff's deputies looked on sympathetically, people began to devise im-

promptu songs in the President's honor, simple ditties
based on the tunes of popular Cuban ballads. A typical
lyric ran:

> *Reagan, Reagan,*
> *Que Dios te*
> *bendiga.*

> Reagan, Reagan,
> May God bless you.

And the fervor was, precisely, that kind of inane religious expression in which even the silliest line is
freighted with commitment.

Arenal told me all of this with the greatest satisfaction and not the slightest hint of irony. For him,
as for most of the Cubans I met in Miami, the only
real question was whether Reagan was strong enough.
In Dade County at the time, Cuban-Americans were
registering nine to one as Republicans. The President
himself was conscious of the esteem in which he was
fiercely if somewhat vaguely held. The year before,
he had given a speech at the Orange Bowl in which
he had praised the veterans of the Bay of Pigs and
referred glowingly, if somewhat mysteriously, to the
famous "Professor Huberto Pardilla." When, on election night, 1984, the returns started to come in and
the extent of the Reagan victory became apparent,
people began to sound their car horns, keeping the
racket up until dawn. With a bread knife, I tapped out
the three short–two long of Algérie Française, the beat
OAS supporters used to sound in the streets of Paris.
Arenal was too flushed with his recollection to notice
and it was, I realized, a cheap thing to do.

But all this Reagan adulation was starting to get on
my nerves. At the American Club, I had noticed a

stack of leaflets exhorting people to sound their horns on October twenty-fifth at 5:30. The leaflet read:

> HISPANICS, CUBANS: Let us support the actions and initiatives of President Ronald Reagan in defense of democratic principles and of the security of America and the rest of the world. Let's all honk our carhorns at 5:30 on October 25th, the date of the liberation of Grenada, to demonstrate that we are present in the fight for freedom and against communism.
>
> Long Live Free Grenada!
>
> Long Live Free Nicaragua!
>
> Long Live Free Cuba!
>
> Long Live Reagan!

Even in Coral Gables, on that night of October 25, I could hear the sound of those car horns, carrying from Eighth Street, across the wide shopping boulevard of the Miracle Mile, down to my open window at the corner of Ponce de Leon and Alcazar. It occurred to me suddenly that my only association with Alcazar was as the site of a heroic stand by a Spanish fascist in Toledo, during the Civil War. The Republicans had threatened that unless this commander surrendered they would shoot his son. The colonel got on the phone and told his son to commend his soul to God and die a martyr. It was all a little close for comfort. Metaphorically, I kept stubbing my toe on these gaudy right-wing pronouncements. Maybe Reagan wasn't Franco but I was in no mood to care. Besides, I suspected the people I was meeting would probably have liked Franco as well. But when I jeered to a young Cuban-American filmmaker over dinner that I saw nothing particularly inspiring about celebrating the victory of seven thousand American combat troops over a hundred and thirty Cuban paramilitary construction workers, he looked at me for a long moment, sighed, and changed the subject.

I was still in this lethal mood when, the next morning, Arenal came to take me to *Unión Radio*. There was a benefit going on for the victims of the recent earthquake in Santiago de Chile. In the street in front of the broadcast center, cars would pull up and disgorge boxes of canned goods, clothes, and medical supplies. Again and again, regular programming was interrupted so that the appeal could go out in support of, as they put it, "the heroic Chilean people." I wondered sourly if the same heroism would be imputed if the earthquake had occurred in North Vietnam. Besides, what was so heroic anyway about walking down the street and having a building fall on your head? Was the Spanish language really as bombastic as it sounded to me that morning or was I simply losing control, giving in to a gift assortment of rancorous feelings? We went inside.

Arenal had wanted me to meet Agustín Tamargo, perhaps the city's most popular Spanish-language talk-show host (later he would defect to Radio Mambí), who was devoting an entire afternoon's program to allow two members of a militant exile group to denounce a guest who had appeared on a previous segment. The man in question, who had arrived in the Mariel boatlift, had had the temerity to declare himself an "anti-Castro leftist." The exiles were there to state that such a thing was simply inconceivable. What was fascinating was not simply the fact that these men found such a proposition preposterous; even the gravel-voiced Tamargo tried to persuade them that their incredulity was — here the host switched for a moment into thickly accented English — "wishful thinking."

[61]

Rather, it was extraordinary to watch such obviously sincere people debate with great heat whether their adversary was a "dupe," an "agent," or a "lackey" of Fidel Castro. This virulent argument was over these, the finest of fine distinctions; one felt the spirit of the Jesuit educations all these men had doubtless undergone, and the inquisitor's intolerance as well.

In retrospect, I suppose that I should have found it peculiar that Arenal, who was only a part-time journalist and not an especially important one, had such easy access to the world of the politically committed exiles of Calle Ocho radio. Every time we would go somewhere, I would protest that we had no appointment, that he should call ahead, that perhaps the trip would be a waste of time. Invariably he would insist, and, with one exception, I cannot remember our being denied an interview. Cuban spontaneity certainly couldn't account for it, but there is something oddly sheeplike about being driven around a strange city, and I did not inquire.

Arenal had told me rather little about his life in Cuba, and I, in turn, had kept my own views rather tightly in check. Certainly I never mentioned to anyone that I had actually been in Havana. Moreover, I had not come to Miami to preach the liberal catechisms of the Upper West Side of Manhattan — even to the extent that I still subscribed to them. I listened, I asked questions, but I said very little. As for the radio stations, their political rhetoric seemed so crude to me that it was easy enough to maintain a kind of dismissive dispassion. As they say in the wine business, these views wouldn't travel; they wouldn't even make it in Washington, where, as I grasped perfectly well even if my new acquaintances didn't, that the President was, anti-Communism-wise at least, more

[62]

sheep than eagle — "Lambo" rather than "Rambo,"
as a cartoonist for the *Buffalo News* had put it.

Then a curious, unsettling thing occurred. During
one of the innumerable station breaks that punc-
tuated the discussion, Arenal, who had been growing
increasingly edgy, shot up from his chair and began
to shout at the panelists. At first, I couldn't make out
very well what he was saying; he was speaking almost
too fast to be intelligible. But I got the gist all right.
He himself had been a political prisoner in Cuba, having served six years. There are countless awful stories
in the world, many if not most far worse than Arenal's, and I suppose that my shock at learning of his
past was as excessive as my rather simple cynicism
about the Calle Ocho had been. But I couldn't help
wondering, as I do now whenever I meet graduates of
Cuba's gulag, whether he had actually been in jail
there while I had been gadding about with those boys
in green field jackets — expressing my solidarity when
I should, at least, have been asking some hard questions. It is perfectly possible after all to believe in the
reality of "anti-Castro leftists" and also to realize that
as far as the Castro regime was concerned it was the
exiles, and not people like me, who had things about
right.

It was in this chastened, somewhat befuddled mood
that I left for New York the following afternoon. Predictably, while I was poring over the morning copy of
El Herald (its headline read, "Cuba Will Match the
U.S. Presence in Nicaragua"; the headline of its Anglo
sister concerned the usual municipal scandal), the
Haitian cabdriver saw an exit that must have reminded him of the airport exit and alighted with pa-
nache a few blocks from the causeway to Miami Beach.
We meandered for several miles before we managed

to find the freeway again. But the detour turned out to be well worth it.

The streets of Miami are remarkably clean, and graffiti, which to a New Yorker are simply the backdrop before which he conducts his business, remarkably rare. Therefore when I saw the beginning of some young thug's public declaration gracing the side of a vacant house, I told the driver to stop. Then I remembered and bellowed, *"Arrêtez ici!"* From the avenue, the visible part of the message, what had caught my eye, had read "U.S. Out" before snaking around the pink stucco wall to the side street side. The full message turned out to be "U.S. Out of the United Nations."

It was, as far as I was concerned, the eighth wonder of the world. Not since the Goldwater campaign of 1964, when a few intrepid daubers had painted his name in some schoolyards (the only really good bit of Goldwater-Miller propaganda was the huge, orientalized image of Barry that grinned down from a billboard in Chinatown; the rest was just scribbling) had I seen right-wing graffiti in America. In New York, if you see the words "U.S. Out," you know what's coming: Nicaragua, Salvador, even America if any Native Americans have passed through — the usual suspects. My return to New York bore this out. The first day back, I stopped in at a bookstore on St. Mark's Place. There by the cash register lay a huge, bowl-shaped receptacle soliciting funds for "the liberated zones of El Salvador and the heroic fighters of the F.M.L.N." I was about to make a joke of it to the clerk when I saw her "Frente Sandinista" T-shirt. I was suddenly ready for another trip to Miami.

6

ON THIS VISIT, I decided, staring myopically out at the runway lights of Miami International, I would not look anyone up. The busy weeks I had spent in New York had done little to dampen the overheated sounds of the Calle Ocho; they were still (the unfortunate image came all too readily to mind) bombing around in my brain. Suddenly, the degree to which I had something in common with Miami Cubans seemed to be getting in the way, and I wanted a degree of anonymity which, so far, I had been unable to secure in Miami. Rather than a seat at the table, and a featured part in the family arguments, I wanted to eavesdrop from behind the kitchen door.

I suspect that it was precisely because I had neither a fixed itinerary nor a list of appointments that this trip was so much more noisome than its predecessor. On the drive in from the airport — curiously, it was the only time I had a Cuban cabdriver take me into town — I found myself overcome by panic at the prospect of being alone in Miami. I remember thinking, my mind seized by a kind of child's literal-mindedness, that I would never succeed in describing the city because, after all, cities were so much larger than people.

Even when I was finally able to dismiss this fancy, I could not shake the feeling of being Gulliver in a Sunbelt Brobdingnag. In my absence, everything seemed to have grown exponentially larger and more assertive. The stanchions of Metrorail were thicker and more densely distributed. As for the downtown high-rises, these no longer appeared simply as buildings, but loomed as huge words, sentences, paragraphs. I do not mean to imply that I had suddenly seen through the glass and steel to the underlying reality of, say, the economic role played by the Barnett Bank in the South Florida real estate market. Far from being able to read between the lines, I was barely legible to myself. Every response, every thought, seemed wrong, or, at best, of surpassing irrelevance. What was this Miami I had thought, so impudently, to describe? In the buildings we were passing, every biographical enormity had taken place. I felt the wind of all imaginable human actions, and, thus, Miami reared up before me, mockingly, in long shot.

Once safely ensconced in my hotel room, I looked out into the bright near-daylight of a downtown Miami evening. Twenty-one stories up in this sumptuous, if half-empty, hotel (in typical Miami fashion, I had no sooner announced my intention of staying there than friends had come forward with lurid rumors about everything from where the marble in the lobby came from to how the land had been acquired), I could stare out my window either at the bay, or, directly across, at the bone-granite facade of an adjacent office tower, its windows like the gun portals of an eighteenth-century warship. On each side of the hotel lay half-excavated construction sites, the future homes — as they say in Chamber of Commerce brochures — of marinas and corporate headquarters. The sublimely named Ima Hogg had once said of Houston, "It will be a nice town if they ever finish it." Houston had nothing on Miami. In sandy pits, the heavy construction machines slept, their sharp ends resting against the ground like the snouts of recumbent dinosaurs.

I spent most of the following day simply lying in bed and ordering up various picturesquely named sandwiches from room service. The discovery that a chicken salad sandwich cost $11.95 and was called "Beachcomber" should, I suppose, have made me more alive to being in Miami. Yet, in a curious way, the safest place to shelter from Florida's "hotel spirit" was, precisely, in a hotel. There is a well-known story of the man who, when the Eiffel Tower was first erected, used to dine regularly in its restaurant. The waiters were mystified, however, by the fact that the man seemed to loathe the food they served. After a week of this, the maître d'hôtel inquired why the man continued to come. "Because," the fellow replied, fury and triumph mingling in his voice, "this is the only vantage point in Paris from which one cannot see this blasted tower." In American hotels, one exists in some sort of generic approximation of middle-class America. The particularities are as absent as they are from network television.

In my room, the television itself rested in a Chinese-looking black lacquered cabinet. Throughout the day, I kept remorselessly flicking the remote control from station to station. Apart from the seeming ubiquity of advertisements by law firms soliciting clients for personal injury suits ("Are you owed money because of someone else's negligence? Then call the firm of Bernstein and Peters . . ."), the images were the same one could have tuned in anywhere else in America. Indeed, if what was on display seemed like what Saul Bellow has justly called "the moronic inferno," the depths in question were national, not regional, down to the ethnically balanced platoon of news readers so reminiscent of those "representative" platoons Van Johnson used to command in movies like *The Battle of the Bulge*.

I suppose it was nothing more than *Schadenfreude*, an itch to see America at its worst, that led me to tune in a program from L.A. called "The New Newlywed Game" rather than to go out into the night air, which, even in the Manhattan-like canyons of downtown Miami, is scented with jasmine. The premise of "The New Newlywed Game" is that four recently married couples are invited on, whereupon each gender in turn (the show, though liberal, is not that liberal) is asked to predict how the other will respond to a series of quaintly risqué questions. Smarmy circumlocutions like "When did you last make whoopee?" for "When did you last make love?" are the order of the day. The contestants invariably seem to be chosen as an accurate reflection of the latest Southern California demographics. There are almost always two white couples, a black couple, and, more often than not, the bright young Asian-Americans who now make up such a large part of middle-class Los Angeles.

For some reason, the questions on the night I watched included one far more concerned with world geography than was prudent. "Which," the host, Bob Eubanks, asked the wives, "is the continent your husband will say his favorite food comes from?" Two of the women replied, "Mexico," a third said, "Italy," and only the fourth managed to summon the ideogram of an actual continent, Asia. When the husbands returned, they proved to be very much of the same opinion as their wives. The first said, "Mexico," and there was the requisite bit of smooching and fist-pumping; the second said, "Italy," and there was more marital harmony. The third respondent, alas, had more or less the brains of a golf divot. Unable to think of a reply, he answered, "L.A." The last couple included the wife, who, unlike the preceeding six adult, gainfully employed, child-expecting (all the women on this particular segment were pregnant) Angelenos, actually knew the difference between a country and a continent. Her husband, however, did not; he answered, "China." The answer was disallowed, and the audience, which clearly did not see why Asia and China were not the same thing, grew visibly mutinous — so much so that Eubanks quickly added that he, after all, warned the contestants their answers would have to match *exactly*.

The television seemed awful because it told one something about what had happened to America. People sounded like they were sending each other singing telegrams, sometimes with a few words left out of the message. The radio was, if anything, worse for what it had to report about Miami. For, if its evidence was to be believed, the city had descended so far into a vortex of resentment, ethnic and racial hatred, futurology, illiteracy, despair, and ignorance, that it might be best to turn everyone into pillars of cocaine and start over.

To be sure, just as television is excessively sanitized (what makes game shows, along with local news, almost unique on TV is that it is one of the few chances one has to see people behaving spontaneously), talk radio, perhaps because it is an anonymous medium, presents a more hateful view of human beings than one ordinarily experiences. The callers often seem not so much to be expressing a view as making an obscene phone call. And if, on the Calle Ocho, I had encountered people whose political opinions were primitive, these English-language broadcasts revealed a human primitivism I had not even imagined.

"Miami," a disgruntled high school teacher had remarked to me on a previous visit, "is a bigot's paradise." Certainly, the airwaves were. On station WINZ, Neal Rogers, one of the best-known if also one of the most controversial talk-show hosts in Miami, seemed obsessed by what he saw as the refusal of Dade County's Hispanics to learn English. One of his callers railed on endlessly about life in this Latin "Banana Republic of Miami" (later, I saw hate mail addressed to Guillermo Martínez, Jr., of the *Miami Herald* franked in the same way). Another caller relied on innuendo. "I think the good old days really were the good old day," he said, adding, quite unnecessarily, "if you know what I mean." On another show, a host gently reproved his guest for having asserted that things in South Florida would turn out well. "I'm an optimist too," the man said, "but it's awfully hard to keep an idea like that up when you live in Miami and you see all this crime and illegal immigration."

The Cubans stuck in Anglo Miami's esophagus like a splintered chicken bone. If there was a drug problem, it was the Cubans' doing; if there was crime, that was their fault too. Guilty, in the eyes of their neighbors, of irreconcilable vices, the Cubans were at once too successful and too big a drain on the public purse. They were also too arrogant, too crafty, too clannish, too insular, and, above all, too goddamn alien. They wouldn't learn English! "It's so nice," said one caller, "to fly up to Birmingham. Everyone speaks English there and is either black or white. You know where you stand in Birmingham."

There was a lot of truth, of course, in what these people were saying, despite the "Phantom of the Opera" presentation. Many of the callers were themselves immigrants or the children of immigrants. Within living memory, they had given up languages and habits of being in order to feel themselves more American. Moreover, they were not given a choice: there was no bilingualism for the Italians when they began to arrive in Tampa around the turn of the century; in the minds of their white Protestant neighbors, they were "Latins" as surely as those bolshevik Cuban cigar makers in nearby Ybor City. But the Italians (and the Jews and the rest) had not expected America to adapt to them, so why were the Cubans so intransigent?

This was the real meaning of what was being said on the radio. Beneath the rancor was a kind of lament. It said: "This isn't fair. We had to change; we did; and now these Cubans don't seem to have to play by the same set of rules." It was true. The rules *had* changed; history and geography had amended the immigrant's contract with the new country. Now, if the Cubans learned English, it would not be out of some ingenuous desire to please, to fit in, but rather because it was in their economic interest to do so, or because they were losing their children, or even because their own sense of American patriotism — something the Miami Anglos could barely credit — called for it. But what the Cubans not only didn't have to do but probably couldn't do was to give Cuba up, at least in the way the Italians, say, had given up Naples.

But no one in Miami, with the exception of some social workers and a few Catholics (whose own partiality toward the new Hispanic immigrants must, however much they denied it, have had some connection to the increased flock the event had brought them), was thinking very clearly. They were in the position of having lied to themselves about themselves for generations. Everything here is simply wonderful, they had said. Come on down, it's perfect here, they had said. Now things clearly were no longer all right, let alone ideal, and Miami was so mentally flaccid, so out of practice at thinking, that every response seemed out of phase.

Indeed, by the sound of the conversations on the radio, Miamians found any kind of thinking something of a trial. There was, for example, the "futurologist" who had gone on one of the better talk shows to plug his book. The man was hardly the second coming of Marshall McLuhan, but after a few minutes it was clear that the host found him far too difficult. With undisguised frustration, he interrupted his guest. "Your ideas seem to require so much thinking," he admonished the man. "We could spend *four* hours on your ideas." It was clear that this was simply an unimaginable project. (I had had several similar encounters in Miami. People would ask where I "found" the time to read, as if, somehow, it was unfair that the whole thing actually required time.)

Thinking how inconceivable such a remark would

have been on the Calle Ocho, I wondered idly if northern Europeans were really meant to live in hot climates. At the University of Miami, a friend had taken me to the Art Museum. A blond boy, heartbreakingly beautiful in his postapocalyptic cutoffs and faintly radioactive-looking orange and green U. of M. T-shirt, entered, Frisbee in hand. What on earth was he supposed to do, I wondered, my eyes flitting between the Renaissance rummage sale on the gallery wall and the blond down on his forearms. I wanted to shout, "Get out of here, Eloi, go back to your vacation."

Many Floridians shared my obsession. When they were not calling up to denounce their Cuban neighbors, they were setting new Olympic records for time spent fretting about the weather. At moments, this took the form of that familiar boastfulness for which Florida is so renowned. "It's eighty-five on the beach," one announcer trumpeted gleefully, "and do you know, folks, they're reporting five below with drifts in Duluth, Minnesota." People genuinely seemed to feel that this represented both an accomplishment on their part, and, simultaneously, the supreme evidence of their good fortune. Either they had forgotten or wished to pretend that they didn't know that it is always cold in Minnesota in the winter and that some people even like it.

In the nineteen-twenties, there had been a cottage industry in Florida devoted to postcards which invidiously compared the balmy South with the frozen North. One showed a group of bathing beauties posed around a gigantic (the suggestion was, perhaps, unintentional), rampantly vertical thermometer whose vertical stripe read eighty-five degrees. "It's just the right temperature in Florida," read the legend. Another postcard showed one group of children forlornly throwing huge, lethal-looking snowballs at one another, while counterposed we see a group of far more benign, happy children running along the beach.

"Come on down, you'll love it," the new Floridians said, but their interest in the weather was not simply civic boosterism but also a way of saying that coming to Florida had not been a mistake. People in Miami are absurdly interested in the temperature, so much so that, on several occasions, I was offered apologies because it had rained. In the eyes of its residents, it was somehow unbearable that Florida be a place like other places, a place one had neither to love absurdly nor to justify. It was precisely the Cubans who were transforming Miami into such a city (their indifference to the weather could be heartwarming after the insistent holidaymaking of Anglo Miami), and the Anglos weren't at all happy.

They bitterly resented the arrival of these Cubans with their drugs, their politics, their Spanish, and their solid sense — made, if anything, stronger by exile — of rootedness. In turn, the Cubans were ideal Morlocks, thinking the Anglos lazy, self-regarding, and spoiled. In turn, these ethnic antagonisms had acted like a magnet for every self-promoting media star in America. During my visit, Phil Donahue was in town, doing a week's worth of programs from the Key Biscayne Marina. Donahue always seems to relish his ability to draw out the worst in people. As he danced around the stage, a combination of Mick Jagger, a parish priest, and a gibbon on Ritalin, he worked a crowd fairly evenly divided between Anglos and Hispanics into a frenzy of pointless, shameful antipathy, which no doubt he would have called therapeutic.

After the show, instead of lynching him, the reporters clustered around asking for advice. And this man, who had almost singlehandedly caused Miami's first middle-class riot, had the temerity to say that, as far as he was concerned, "we just can't afford to get so mad at each other." Good, Phil.

When I returned to the hotel from my afternoon in the tropics with Donahue, I ran into a local reporter whom I had interviewed on my last visit. I told her about the scene in Key Biscayne and she nodded grimly. "It's terrible," she said. We went to talk about what was happening in Miami, about the upcoming film festival and the rumors, then proliferating in the city, that the Duvalier regime in Haiti might be about to fall. Surprisingly, for the Haitians are disliked by almost everyone else in Miami, this woman was intent on singing their praises. "They're wonderful people," she said, "so grateful." Her charity had a sting in its tail, for she added matter-of-factly, "You won't see them acting like Cubans." I suggested, as gently as I could, that the Cubans really had very little to feel grateful for, but she simply fixed me with a frozen, pained smile and repeated that she thought the Haitians were "so nice." It was as if she had been talking about an exotic pet.

When I regained my room, I reminded myself that I was, after all, in Florida — a state where neither altruism nor decent race relations are old traditions. This was the land of let the buyer beware and an intractably segregated school system (in the nineteen-thirties, there were only five accredited black high schools in the entire state). Beneath this gleaming, tropical Wall Street was another, harsher city. Money might have altered the skyline, and migration the ethnic mix, but Miami was still the same tough, bitter town it had been when the Jim Crow laws had prevailed and Meyer Lansky and Santo Trafficante had run the mob, both in South Florida and in Havana, from the marble hotel lobbies of Miami Beach.

Moreover, the people who worked in these new banks and corporate headquarters were themselves not immigrants so much as transients. The average (Anglo) business family stays in Miami for no more than five years before being reassigned elsewhere. Their experience, during their stay, was of a homogeneous subdivision, the drive to and from work on the freeway, office life, and what they heard about Miami in the media. But on the radio and on television, Miami was perpetually presented as either Tahiti or Beirut, and presented in words which no one could possibly make sense of. Euphemisms one had assumed were an aberration of Army English seemed to have permeated every level of discourse. If there had been fog at the airport, this was reported as "dense fog created limited visibility last night in Dade County." When a sportscaster was asked by a colleague to predict the outcome of an upcoming bowl game, he replied by confessing: "Well, I don't know much about Texas A&M. I am from Texas, but I've been here a few years and so I've lost my roots." I wanted to offer to help him look for them.

Predictably, most of the news broadcasts were devoted to crime. After the reality of the horrors themselves would come joke remarks or exculpatory statements that would bathe the facts in a solvent of mind-deadening babble. When, for example, Ken Nelson, the president of the Miami Fraternal Order of Police, was asked to explain why so many cops were being arrested on criminal charges, all he could muster was "It has to do with the area here, I mean the amount of crime that comes through this area."

Not that Nelson wasn't correct. In recent years, scarcely a month has gone by in Miami without a new police scandal. In a town like Miami, it is almost surprising that some enterprising broker isn't offering felony insurance to cops. Certainly, the felony indictments have been raining down on the station houses — something police spokesmen keep insisting is a healthy sign since it means the department is "cleaning its own house." On the evening news, I watched the latest indictment. Three cops had, it appeared, broken up a drug deal on a boat in the Miami River. But, rather than acting like Crockett and Tubbs, the D.A. said, these men had killed the dealers and stolen the cocaine.

The case was only one in a line of push-in robberies, break-ins, fencing operations, car thefts, extortions (one on a fellow officer about whom other rumors were circulating). The Miami police department gave the impression that it had taken the criminal code out for a test drive. It reminded me of the opening scene of Sergio Leone's *The Good, the Bad, and the Ugly*, where Eli Wallach stands on the scaffold listening balefully as the endless list of his crimes is read out to him. In the movie, Wallach is rescued by his partner Clint Eastwood before he swings, just as the audience knows he will be. And Miami seemed to be developing a fairly similar expectation of its criminal justice system.

Nonetheless, it was difficult, except in a few neighborhoods in Miami, really to believe that it was a dangerous city. In New York, late at night, one hears the *musique concrète* of police sirens, the scream of an ambulance, a bottle crashing, a curse. In pristine downtown Miami, there were no graffiti, the air was fragrant, a breeze was blowing off the bay, and the silence, far from being menacing, seemed immensely healing after the electronic noise I had been attending to. I walked along the edge of the water for almost a mile, not seeing a soul. When I returned to the hotel, the Guatemalan night manager was frantic with reproach. "Don't you know how dangerous it is out there?" he pleaded, then, lapsing into Spanish, said commandingly, "Don't go out there." I went apologetically off to my room. Later, I stared out at the city, imagining every unspeakable horror.

7

EVERYONE, except writers and journalists, wants to travel innocently when they go abroad. If they are honest, no one feels the same way about traveling at home. This is why a few scattered terrorist incidents in Europe during the summer of 1986 persuaded so many Americans that foreign travel was unsafe and why a series of well-publicized, racially motivated killings in Trinidad in the mid-nineteen-seventies almost destroyed that country's holiday trade. The fact that it was, statistically, safer to spend one's entire vacation flying back and forth between Athens and Cairo than to walk around at night in most major American cities made little difference. What happened at home formed a part of what was loosely conceived of as "life"; if an untoward event happened, there was nothing very much anyone could do. In contrast, what happened abroad happened "out of context," and, hence, outside the rigors of daily life; such an interruption was perceived with bottomless resentment.

Domestic resorts were really no different. The tourists who flocked there were just as intent on getting away from daily life, not encountering it, in its starker manifestations, in unfamiliar surroundings. The bad publicity that Miami began to receive in the late nineteen-seventies carried the damaging message that the city was a real place. In going there, one was no longer simply getting away. This was what had the Chamber of Commerce people so scared. It was all very well to treat the rest of the world like a zoological garden (Africa), an old curiosity shop (Europe), or like a house of horrors (the Middle East), but now Miami was getting the same treatment. And yet, despite the new banks and the drug money, the city remains dependent on tourism.

In the nineteen-fifties and nineteen-sixties, the money came from the so-called snowbirds, prosperous Northerners who wintered in Florida, and, particularly, the Jews who had retired to Miami Beach. In the nineteen-seventies, as Miami became more and more a Hispanic city, vacationers from Latin America picked up the slack. This was the era of the oil boom in Venezuela. The tourists came up from Caracas in convoys, their riotously overvalued bolivares aching to be spent. The Venezuelan tourist became a stock figure in Miami, his only analogue the Arab sheikh loose in the West End of London. Merchants dubbed them *Deme Dos*, "give me two," and, indeed, they spent like crazy, buying up condominiums on such fashionable streets as Brickell Avenue as well as consumer goods in record quantities.

In Caracas, there was even a successful film made about the annual pilgrimage to Miami. The plot of *Adíos Miami* concerns a successful young builder who, to impress his girl friend, takes her to Florida. When they arrive, they begin to do the town until, one morning, a telegram arrives from Caracas informing our hero that his partner has absconded with the company funds and he's broke. The girl abandons him, he's kicked out of his hotel, and the bulk of the picture shows him trying to work his way back to Venezuela. He can't find work because Cubans, according to the film, will only hire other Cubans, and it goes without saying that the Venezuelan version of Miami presents the city as another Latin-American capital. The film was, interestingly enough, made the year after the president of Ecuador made his famous remark about Miami being the capital of Latin America.

But Miami could not retain its Latin-American tourists because their currencies could not retain much value. When the comedy (of OPEC, not *Adíos Miami*) was over and the bolivar had gone down the tubes, the city found itself in need of a new set of free spenders. Unfortunately, this was precisely the moment when that series of tourist-repellant events began to unleash themselves over Dade County. The drug murders and Mariel got most of the headlines. More subtly aversive, perhaps because they were less threatening than they were pathetic, were the Haitian boat people.

Haiti is the poorest country in the Western Hemisphere. For thirty years, it was the bruised fiefdom of the Duvalier family (though it was such an impoverished tyranny that even after "Papa Doc" Duvalier had proclaimed himself "President For Life," he continued to use his old stationery before it was exhausted, adding neatly in his own hand the words "*à vie*" after the title President). Over a hundred thousand Haitians braved the seas between Hispaniola and Miami between 1965 and 1980. They claimed to be fleeing political oppression, and, though of course many were, still more were doubtless doing what immigrants have always done — going where there is work. Miami became to Haitians what Los Angeles has become to the rural poor of Mexico . . . Oz.

The panic in a Miami reeling from the cocaine wars and hotels suddenly bereft of Venezuelans was considerable and ugly. It was, in fact, at the insistence of Florida's governor, Bob Graham, that the Coast Guard began a serious attempt to intercept the Haitian illegals. The year before, the Immigration and Naturalization Service constructed, at the edge of the Everglades, the huge Krome internment center, destination for those Haitians who didn't manage to make it to Miami's Little Haiti, or the other, smaller communities throughout Dade and Broward counties. Krome is an ulcer in Miami; apart from a few civil liberties activists and Haitian community leaders like Father Gérard St. Juste (the name, though too good to be true, is real), it is never mentioned — as taboo a subject at dinner as one's recent colostomy or a new recipe for broiled dachshund.

Apart from the journalist I had met, almost no one in Miami seemed to have a decent word for these Haitians. It was almost as if they were too much to think about, just as so many white Americans who have finally managed to pay attention to blacks find the whole issue of Hispanics beyond their neurological threshold. As for Miami Cubans, they were, if anything, more vitriolic about Haitians than were the Anglos. Race is a loaded question within the Cuban community. They had already had Mariel, which had been a bucket of cold water on their image of what Cubans were. As a friend of mine put it, "We had invented a Cuba in which everyone was white. When the *marielitos* came, we were forcibly reminded that Cuba is not a white island, but, largely, a black one."

Many Cubans expressed this wonderment at how many blacks had come over from Mariel (as blacks say in Cuba, "Being a white man is a full-time job"). In the twenty-seven years Cubans had lived in Miami, the mutual antipathy between themselves and American blacks had far outstripped the more restrained animosities that separated Cuban and Anglo. American blacks, many Cubans said to me privately, were at the bottom because they belonged there. Batista's Cuba was, after all, a hierarchical place. As for the Haitians, they were animals.

For me, despite my almost curatorial relation to Third World taxi drivers, the Haitians were simply a huge surprise. We all make mental maps of the places we are about to visit, and they are, inevitably, quite intensely parochial. There is a marvelous Saul Steinberg drawing that parodies New York insularity by presenting a map of Manhattan island, shown in rigorous detail and followed by an absurdly compressed continent (Chicago can, I believe, be dimly apprehended), that only expands to encompass that single other bit of the North American land mass credible to New Yorkers: California. In Miami, they were selling a takeoff in which a detailed rendering of the Caribbean was followed by the Keys, and then, center stage, by Miami itself. After that, there is only a thumb's width worth of South separating Jacksonville, Florida, from New York.

I had, of course, been diligent; but I was discovering that my own cartoon seemed to have room only for Cubans and Anglos pitted against each other (with remote nods to Northern Jews and American blacks). It was turning out that while I had been monitoring the airwaves and crisscrossing the city in search of this bilingual battle between Gog and Magog, I had missed other, equally interesting, stories. Certainly, I had missed the Haitians, who, if they figured at all, were little more than the amiable incompetents who chauffered me from airport to hotel, from Anglo to Cuban to valium.

When I first read a newspaper account of a local high school that was said to number "white, Cuban, black, and Haitian students," I put this down to reportorial heatstroke. When I heard that there had been serious talk of making the signs on the Metrorail system trilingual in English, Spanish, and French (and what a surprise that would have been to the patois-reading Haitian ridership), I thought I had uncovered another bit of inept, though well-intentioned, civic exercise in "multiculturalism" (take three, they're small). My more paranoid Cuban friends put it all down to an attempt by the Anglo establishment to ridicule bilingualism by using the Haitians as a ruse — a sort of "If it isn't English only it will be Babel" position. It was hard to imagine the Haitians, so quiet was their everyday demeanor, as a forceful presence in Miami.

The night the U.S. State Department gave Jean-Claude "Baby Doc" Duvalier his walking papers, I couldn't sleep. During the deepest hours before dawn, racked by that half-somnolence in which every sickly fancy takes its turn, I bobbed in and out of consciousness, read, furiously stabbed the radio on and off. Finally, still well before dawn, I abandoned for good the idea of sleep and began to twist the AM dial looking for something soothing to listen to. In New York, at that hour, the classical stations play sacred music. When I hear it, I tend to think dimly of once more trying to become a Christian, or, alternatively, of taking up cigarettes again. Either the Miami classical station hadn't yet come on the air or I couldn't find it. Instead, Cuban newsreaders were announcing peremptorily that the military had formed a provisional government in Port-au-Prince and that the Duvaliers and their entourage had been landed, courtesy of the U.S. Air Force, in the mountains of eastern France. In Miami's Little Haiti, the announcer continued, people seemed to be dancing in the streets.

I succeeded in clumsily throwing on my clothes and hopping down the hall to the elevator banks. Outside, Miami was already warm in the predawn light. A lone cabdriver dozed peacefully at the taxi rank, reminding me, absurdly, of a businessman at an opera gala snoozing his way through the heavier bits of *Tristan*. I jumped in, noting to my relief that the driver's name was Jean-Baptiste Dieudonné. Did his friends ever call him "Dieu"? We set off for Little Haiti.

At 54th and Biscayne Boulevard, the police cordons began. The week before, a pro-Duvalier Haitian had backed a car into an anti-Duvalier crowd, and somebody had been killed. This time, the Miami cops were taking no chances. There were knots of them staring impassively out of their mirrored shades, and I saw a couple of sharpshooters crouched on the roof of an adjacent supermarket. There were camera crews moving in and out, looking for politicians to interview. I squeezed past the armored hips of two Dade County sheriff's deputies, and there before me was a carnival.

People were still rubbing the sleep from their eyes as they came out of their houses, but within moments they were dancing. Duvalier had changed the Haitian national colors from blue and red to black and red, and so everyone was in blue and red, even if all they could muster was a scrap of fabric or even, improbably, a fat square of cobalt-blue linoleum. At first the crowd was small, lone men and women dancing to music they alone could hear. Then, groups began to form, the mass of people growing thicker and more jubilant by the moment. An enormous middle-aged woman, her face partly covered in two towels, one red, the other blue, lunged ecstatically toward the police line, screaming: "When I hear Jean-Claude he gone, I fly like a bird." Then she toppled back into the crowd.

By nine A.M., the steel bands were in the streets and no one needed internal music to keep the beat. I heard a woman shout, "Thank you, God, thank you, God," and a man, weeping, repeat over and over, "I love my country." The joy of the crowd was hysterical, inarticulate, overwhelming. By noon, the music was deafening and I could see dancers fainting in ungainly heaps while others danced over them. In the distance, the ambulance sirens kept up a steady whine. As I crossed back to where the TV camera trucks were parked, I heard a reporter say, cheerily, "Little Haiti traffic is blocked at Northeast Second Avenue and Fifty-fourth Street for the celebration." It was rush hour; they had been dancing since before sunrise.

Cars went past, mostly poor, battered vans, horns honking madly. From open windows, shirtless black men waved the blue and red colors of the Republic of Haiti. The conga line of dancers still snaked, its thirst for celebration unquenched, through the miserable streets of Little Haiti. It had become a demonstration, though of what I could not be sure, and it was impossible to watch the black fists waving in the sun, the songs, the banners, the improvised chanting, and not think of Soweto. In Little Haiti, though, it was black people winning for once, and poor people exulting. A man shouted into a camera, "I've been waiting for this for twenty-six years." And the Cuban cop next to me muttered, "So have I." The fall of a dictator is a moment of irrepressible happiness.

It had begun to rain, and, though this did nothing to quiet the crowd, I had had enough. Every Haitian in the city seemed to have taken the day off and there wasn't a cab to be found, but there were plenty of limousines parked at the edge of the festivities — all the politicians had arrived by midafternoon — and for thirty bucks one of the drivers agreed to run me into Little Havana. As we drove, the rain became thicker, more punishing. There was no traffic along the Calle Ocho, except for the occasional misplaced Haitian-driven van, trying to approximate the sound of "À bas Duvalier" on the horn. The limousine left me off in front of a restaurant called the Centro Vasco. The TV at the bar was on; not unexpectedly, I heard a Spanish announcer narrating the events in Little Haiti.

Next to the television, a group of middle-aged Cuban businessmen were morosely discussing the day's events. The fall of someone else's dictator, as the Cuban cop had been saying, is not a moment of irrepressible happiness. Turning to me, one of the men said flatly — what else could there be to talk about? — "The Haitians may learn to be sorry. We were all happy when Batista fell and now look!"

The TV showed an earnest commentator. He said,

"President Reagan, what about our beloved Cuba?" The men at the bar nodded, but while there was fervor, I could discern little hope in their voices. Feeling like an uninvited guest at a wake, I paid and slipped out of the bar. The streets of Little Havana seemed, if anything, even gloomier than before.

Back at the hotel, I watched as the local stations replayed yet again the dancers and celebrants of Little Haiti. Everyone was wondering whether, now that Duvalier had gone, the Haitians would return to the island. It didn't seem likely. Despite what the civil liberties lawyers said, there were, in fact, relatively few political exiles compared to the tens of thousands of people who had come illegally to Florida for work. The other view had been a polite fiction, little more. Every young Haitian interviewed seemed set on staying. One said, "I'd like to visit." Another girl smiled and said softly, "I want to be a nurse." Looking at the day's events on television, it was remarkable to see how foreign the Haitians became as they danced, and how American the Cuban-American cops seemed as they watched, their faces masks of First World disdain for the antics of Third World people.

As I drifted off to sleep, I heard the Haitian news give way for a moment to an account of the Philippine election. There was a report from Manila, and then, at greater length, interviews with some members of what was described as "the Filipino community in Dade County." They were cautiously optimistic about the return of democracy. The next segment featured an interview with the director of the Miami Convention Bureau. He said, "Miami is the newest, and probably the most glamorous American City."

*   *   *

Mornings in a Miami hotel bring tropical light and the *Miami Herald*. It was Sunday, and, thumbing quickly past the headlines about Duvalier and Marcos (I couldn't face them again), I immersed myself in the Travel section. The lead story began: "Togo: This tiny West African country beckons in winter with sunny beaches and fine French food." Below this, there was a badly reproduced photograph of a black child in a sketchy sarong carrying an even younger black child in some sort of floral-print bundle. The older girl stared squarely at the camera with a gaze so knowing I was surprised the photo editor had let it pass. Adulthood was already present in the lines distinctly etched at the corners of her mouth. The infant on her back looked more cheerful, time, as Dickens says in *Dombey and Son*, not yet having worked its deeper operations.

Besides the Togo story, the two other features were the unfortunately titled "White, White World of Yellowstone" and "Going Gets Steep for the Handicapped." Too true. I turned back to the photograph of the two Togolese children. Cleverly, the background came out completely fuzzy. One could discern a shimmer of sun, and beneath it what seemed like an Impressionist's allusion to a hut and some trees. In the article itself, there was much talk of dancing and of cultural diversity. A satisfied visitor from South Florida reported: "I stumbled onto a festival. The street was filled with people dancing; everyone was dressed in white. I felt welcome to stay."

The travel writer advised that tourists would like Togo. It was "a mellow, friendly place that welcomes the stranger, called *yovo*. The country is so small yet so diverse that you can see savannah, jungle, mountains, and seacoast, and many of the forty different tribal cultures, in just a few days." Hurriedly, I tossed the Travel section toward the end of the bed and reached for Home and Design. I read, "Houses tell stories, some happy, others sad. . . . The story of *Mi Encanto* (Spanish for My Dream) goes back half a century. . . . *Mi Encanto* was built by Edmund E. Allyne, inventor of the kerosene refrigerator, for his wife Mildred, when they learned that she had a terminal illness. . . . The architect, Marion Wyeth, had been a pupil of Addison Mizner." I asked for political asylum in the Sports section.

8

HOME HAS ALWAYS BEEN for me an idea as difficult as it is beguiling. Part of this feeling, I have no doubt, comes from the biographical fact that I don't so much come from a nuclear family as from a sub-atomic one. As a result, I remain irrationally jealous of anyone who boasts a large, close-knit family; irrationally jealous and immediately fascinated. I have spent most of my life trying to find just such a family to graft myself onto — like a barnacle looking for a battleship. What is less easy for me to explain is why I have habitually aimed these longings at people who themselves scarcely fit in: homosexuals, foreigners, exiles.

Exiles, particularly, have always struck me as living with such a peculiar, enviable intensity that the normal melodramas of family life pale by comparison. To be sure, this is at best only a part of the story. I am well aware of the moral dangers of sentimentalizing the dispossessed. When one does this in one's own country, there is the added risk that what is being engaged is, in reality, the jaded taste for exoticism. What better show, after all, than quarrels not one's own? This may have been why I almost always felt more comfortable in Miami among Cubans, or even Haitians, than among Anglos of any persuasion. Travel is a form of appropriation, an act of collecting experiences, and I knew enough already about the barbecues in West Kendall, or, for that matter, conversations about the Middle East in the Jewish delicatessens of Miami Beach, to feel little interest in them, acquisitive or otherwise. It was not that I thought the future was.with the Hispanics. I don't think the future is with anybody. I simply felt more comfortable, creaturally, on the Calle Ocho.

After the celebrations in Little Haiti, however, I had had enough of alien histories, and of the Third World in general, at least in its tragic aspect. During my next several visits to Miami, I tried to avoid all that like the plague (of which, curiously, there had been an outbreak in the miserable migrant town of Belle Glade). The sensation was, almost literally, one of being sated, of having taken in more than I could digest. I wanted to return to the official Miami of gorgeous days and bourgeois bank balances, of striving entrepreneurs and new foreign cars lovingly tended. This didn't necessarily mean Anglos. I simply longed to see the establishment, any establishment. Dusting off my American Express card, I went off in hot pursuit.

On the drive out to Coral Gables, the news was mostly a weather report. There had been seven inches of snow in New York the night before, and the weather man asked brazenly, "Aren't you glad we live here?" I stared quizzically at the back of the cabdriver's head. He was nodding. After a time, he seemed to tire of the news, or, perhaps, of assent, and slipped a cassette into a small, dented tape player, which rested on the front seat next to him. The music that came squeaking out was by some Country and Western religious group. When they sang about Jesus taking care of all your needs, the driver sang along. In a heavy Creole accent, he repeated, "Jesus will provide for me." The man maintained a frigid silence when the singers intoned about sacrifice and trouble. No doubt he'd had enough of that without anyone else's help.

The cab let me off at the corner of Ponce and Minorca, alongside the Southeast Bank building. It appeared as if there was another religious ceremony taking place there. A truck was parked in the side street and young executives in white shirts and ties with dancing protozoa on them were unloading boxed IBM personal computers. The work took place in complete silence — a Sicilian saint's day or a Masai wedding without the audio. Like African women, the junior execs lifted the boxes onto their heads and, in double rank, proceeded into the office tower. I noticed that, like so many office workers in Miami, they all wore little beepers. None went off. Not until the last Arrow-shirted back had disappeared behind the tinted glass doors was I able to turn away and head for my lunch date. It was at a French restaurant called Le Festival, a little further up toward Miracle Mile. As I entered, it was the sort of place in which the atmosphere was honed to a fine degree of "authenticity"; in other words, it was another Florida theme park, the theme this time being French food. The Hispanic maître d'hôtel greeted me in an approximation of French that would have convinced only his mother and led me toward my lunch date, Ambler Moss.

I knew Moss already. If anyone epitomized both an upbeat and an intelligent view of what was going on in Miami, it was he. Moss was a Yale graduate, a former submarine officer, and State Department desk officer. He had resigned to practice international law in Brussels, only to return to the Foreign Service, during the Carter administration, as ambassador to Panama. During the Canal Treaty negotiations, Moss had become friendly with the Panamanian dictator (a word that made him wince when I used it), Omar Torrijos. It was widely asserted in Washington that, more than anyone, Moss had handled the so-called back channel discussions with the Panamanians. Many credited him with having saved the treaty when agreement seemed hopeless.

Now Moss was director of the Graduate School of International Studies at the University of Miami. He had been recruited there by Edward Foote, a fellow Yalie and the new president of the university, one of a number of talented people who had been persuaded to try to lift the school out of its mediocrity. There was reason for hope. Though the student body remained primeval, the faculty — particularly in law, where the University of Chicago had been very successfully raided and various Marxist critical-theory types carried off like rare orchid cuttings — was improving. It would continue to do so, Moss insisted. "Miami," he said in response to my exuberant left eyebrow, "can often seem like a sixteen-year-old: perfectly grown-up one week, then suddenly childish the next."

As I was trying to calculate how many times since Oscar Wilde people had called America an adolescent country, the waiter interrupted. The usual Miamian linguistic farce took place, with the Cuban waiter addressing us in his fractured French, Moss, ever the diplomat, responding in flawless Castilian, I, sullenly refusing to play, ordering in my brusquest Parisian, whereupon, splendidly, the waiter repeated everything back to us in Cuban-accented English. Dripping from this trip through Miami's mangle of idioms (it must have been a record for ways to pronounce *coquilles St. Jacques* in a single conversation), we returned to higher education. Moss, I felt, dimly regretted that we were no longer speaking Spanish. For, when he had realized the waiter was Cuban (there must, after all, be a few French waiters in Miami), he had slid into Spanish like a man crawling back under his comforter on a cold, pretty weekend morning.

All of a sudden, I saw Moss as cast very much in the mold of those sixteenth-century English recusants, who, rather than betray their faith, had chosen Philip II and Catholic Spain over an England ruled by Elizabeth I. It was not the first time in Miami that, dimly, tantalizingly, the ghost ships of the Armada had insinuated themselves in my mind. This week the city was celebrating Hispanic Heritage Week. The warships of the Duke of Medina Sidonia may not have made it to Dover, but, as the brochure noted, they had disembarked along the Miami River in the sixteenth century. Flyers all over town showed a cartoon conquistador on a hobby horse blowing a trumpet. In the lobby of the *Miami Herald* building, there was a map of the United States with the lower third marked as former Spanish possessions. "If Spain had not existed 400 years ago," the legend read, "there would have been no United States today." And if your aunt had wheels she'd be a bus, I thought, at the same time realizing that this was an old undercurrent in American history, suddenly given new force by the massive Hispanic immigration of our time. Fifty years ago, the philosopher Josiah Royce wrote an essay in which he treated the Mexican-American War as a continuation in the New World of the battle between Protestant England and Catholic Spain.

Which side, I wondered idly, would Moss be on today? It was, to be sure, a fanciful thought to entertain in modern-day Miami, a town which epitomized Calvin Coolidge's immortal remark that the business of America is business. Nonetheless, I could not shake the thought that Moss's way of being, his conception of what he found compelling about his own country, must have subtly shifted since he had come to Miami — particularly in the Latin Miami, where he preferred to spend his time. Perhaps mine had, too, although to what I couldn't say. As for Moss, he did seem aware that something new had happened to him. He told me, boastfully and matter-of-factly at once, that in his car he only tuned in the classical music or the Spanish-language stations. His wife, he added (she is Sumner Welles's granddaughter), believed him to be a different person when he spoke Spanish. "She says I lose all my WASP hang-ups," he said laughingly.

No doubt Moss had chafed, during his years as a diplomat, at having to play the role of the professional "gringo." As an intelligent man, he certainly knew just how parochial the view of the world from Washington really was. By choosing to come to Miami, he had swung one hundred eighty degrees in the other direction, and had opted for a role in creating the new bilingual, bicultural city of the Chamber of Commerce's fondest imaginings. According to this view it wasn't that the Cubans were taking over Miami, but rather, as Frank Soler had put it, that "the world was taking over and the city becoming an international megalopolis." If one scratched the bombast (megalopolis was a word straight out of the World of the Future exhibit at the 1939 World's Fair), the boosters had a point. As a cultivated man, Moss was of the view that the only hope for real culture in South Florida was through the area's connection with Latin America. Anything else would leave Miami a poor imitation of New York or Los Angeles. "I want young Cuban-Americans to speak Spanish," Moss said in an unguarded moment, "because I think it will bring a little culture here."

This was not all that different from the stance of young Cuban-American intellectuals like Ricardo Pau-Llosa, who had written, "As far as art is concerned, Miami belongs to the Latin Americans." Pau-Llosa went on to argue that the artistic models for Latin America had, traditionally, come from Europe and not the United States. And the Latin Miami to which Moss seemed so drawn was as much European as anything else. It was, no doubt, Europe in embryo, but, for Miami's boosters the metaphor of Miami as infant, far from being demoralizing, was itself reason for hope. "We're still in diapers," Frank Soler told me. "Just wait ten years." Miami would become, over time, the ideal place for the twenty-first-century cosmopolitan. To be sure, as both Moss and Soler were prepared to concede, most Miami Cubans remained blissfully untouched by any effete impulses toward cultural benefactions. In fact, they were aggressively philistine, as Cuban artists and writers who had sought support in the community were all too aware. But Miami's boosters were persuaded that this, like adolescence, was only a phase the city was going through.

I was not so sanguine. One of the more interesting contrasts in style between the boosterism of Ambler Moss and that of Frank Soler was that Moss, for whatever reason, seemed genuinely interested in culture, while for Soler, as for so many successful Cuban-Americans, culture seemed largely to connote either some sort of ethnic success or the classier manifestation of civic triumphalism. There was no clear differentiation between, say, an art gallery, and the acquisition of a major league baseball team for Miami. They were both adornments, signs the city had "arrived."

Soler himself seemed prone to conflate newness and grandeur. "I am awed," he told me, "by the grandeur of Vienna's Staatsoper and I'm absolutely appalled by the peeling paint in the Dade County Civic Center." Cubans might view themselves as proto-Europeans, but, in fact, they looked all but soldered at the joints to the American cult of the new. In New York or in Paris, people in the arts are uncomfortable (though nothing more) with certain outward manifestations of their own bourgeois prosperity. The credit cards fit in frayed trouser pockets; the expensive restaurants strive to look informal. In Miami, in contrast, the effort seems entirely in the opposite direction. When Ricardo Pau-Llosa came to collect me at my hotel for the first time, I was somewhat taken aback by his shiny new Volvo and businessman's sports jacket. His counterpart elsewhere would have felt some vestigial unease at not appearing more bohemian. As for Pau-Llosa, he shook me warmly by the hand, offered me a cigar, and drove me off to lunch in his spanking new Volvo. While it is true that Matisse said painters should dress like bank clerks, the effect is nonetheless a startling one when glimpsed on a mass scale.

Both Soler and Moss had made much of the fact that a new "international school" had recently been founded in Miami. Certainly, it was altogether a good thing for as many Cuban-Americans as possible to be weaned from the Catholic schools and military academies they had favored in the nineteen-sixties — the kind of place where, as one former teacher put it, "they teach nothing but God, country, and short hair." When Soler had told me about the school, he had pointed to a photo of his daughter, an exquisitely beautiful blonde child, and said, "She will be completely multicultural. Children with backgrounds in South Florida will be the ones to maintain the U.S. place in the world. They'll be able to compete abroad because they'll feel comfortable abroad."

For Soler the principal interest of multiculturalism seemed to be business. For Moss, I felt, the rewards were more mixed. Certainly one of them was the opportunity to do something new; another, I thought, was precisely the foreign feel of Miami, the sense of being abroad at home. I liked this too. At a dinner party on Brickell Avenue, it was possible, provided one kept one's back resolutely toward the sea, to believe oneself in Madrid. The concierge in the lobby greeted one in Spanish; upstairs, everything from the Rioja and the *tapas* to the mustachioed maid seemed "Made in Spain." Moreover, as I sat talking with Moss, I realized that to him Miami had the attraction of being a new synthesis, a chance to meld the pleasures of Europe with the sportier thrills of life in the American Sunbelt. This is imaginable only in Miami. In Houston, for example, it is often possible to imagine oneself in Guadalajara, Mexico, but never in Barcelona, Spain, whereas in Miami, Moss could boast of having been on his boat only that morning, and, however much I remained persuaded that Tahiti would win out over Salamanca, the picture was an attractive one.

After lunch, we drove downtown for a brandy at one of Moss's favorite Cuban restaurants. A huge, nearly Day-Glo oil painting of Ernest Hemingway in a *guayabera* guarded the entry hall. Images of Hemingway rank right after portraits of Martí and Maceo in the iconography of Little Havana. In this one, "Papa" looked like a Buddhist temple dog. Further on, crossed U.S. and Cuban flags hung along the walls, illuminated like votaries. During the drive I had been wondering whether, by "brandy," Moss meant Spanish brandy or cognac. In Miami, I had discovered, if you want the latter you must say so. We did. To my relief, the Hispanicization of Ambler Moss had not proceeded to that extreme.

At the bar, an old man sat poised over his rum and tonic, occasionally glancing stoically at the television, from which images of dancing Haitians came flickering back at him. We had barely been served when the man looked at us keenly and inquired if we spoke Spanish. Moss brightened visibly. For the next half hour, I listened as Moss and the old man talked. Mostly, they traded proverbs of the "Man proposes, God disposes" variety. Old men like formulas; so do fellow travelers of any stripe. Moss's wife was right: he was transformed in Spanish. He began to gesture freely with his hands, to use laughter as a punctuation to his sentences, and even to swear a bit, something I had never heard him do in English.

I shut my eyes briefly. As I did so, I could hear nothing in the abstraction of sound unaccompanied by sight except the Spanish language, cascading about me in all its manic, overstressed ebullience. The sensation was not at all like what one can experience in Mexican East L.A. (where, in any event, it is unwise to shut one's eyes for too long). There one feels like a somewhat insecure rajah waiting for the moment when the peasants will revolt. In Miami, I felt both more secure and more like a foreigner, a traveler set down in some unaccountably misplaced piece of Iberia or, perhaps, in the Southern Cone of South America. We might have been in a bar in Buenos Aires, which was, I had come to suspect, a good part of the appeal the place held for Ambler Moss.

A group of fit-looking young Latin-Americans (they were far too Indian-looking to possibly be Cubans) sat eating at a nearby table. Their T-shirts all read, "Paraguay," although, as I cautioned myself, in an era where the Amal militiamen holding the American hostages in Beirut sported Barry Manilow, Bruce Springsteen, and "Airborne, Death from Above" on their chests, it was important not to race to conclusions. For all I knew, "Paraguay" was the name of a band from San Juan, Puerto Rico. But, as Moss quickly determined, these kids were indeed Paraguayan soccer players, part of the national squad, that had come up to play an exhibition game against a team from Medellín, Colombia.

One flushed, almost steaming European face stood out among all those coppery Indian physiognomies. The man in question had the authority of fit late middle-age; he seemed to be diagramming a play with the aid of wineglasses and salt and pepper shakers. I couldn't quite hear what he was saying to the players, but Moss whispered in my ear, "If he's the coach, then I'll bet the team is bilingual in Guarani and German." I nodded, but Moss had in fact made a remarkable statement; not about Paraguay but about Miami. For although our exchange could easily have taken place anywhere in Latin America, I suspected that it could have happened nowhere in the United States except in Miami.

In New York or Washington, one practically needed to be an expert in Latin-American affairs to know that the dictator of Paraguay is called Alfredo Stroessner, the son of German immigrants, or that in most parts of that country they speak Guarani, not Spanish. But what would have been fairly arcane information even for fairly well-informed readers of good national newspapers like the *New York Times* and the *Washington Post* was as elementary as eighth-grade civics in Hispanic Miami. The city didn't need any annual Hispanic Heritage Festival to "maintain" Miami's Latin heritage. Indeed, if anything was in danger of falling down the memory hole in Dade County, it was, as some hysterical Anglos correctly presumed, Atlanta, not Asunción.

Where else in the United States but Miami would seem like a logical place for a team from Paraguay to come to play an opponent from Colombia? In New York, no one would have paid any attention because no one would care; in Miami, everyone simply took it for granted. Where else could the game be played so that all of Latin America could see it on television? Certainly not Mexico, which had managed, during the recent World Cup, to hopelessly botch TV transmission to a hundred countries. As for the players, they, though country boys all, certainly did not act as if they were in an unfamiliar setting, though, of course, it was highly unlikely any of them had been in Miami before. It must have sounded as much to them like Latin America in that restaurant as it did to me.

Finally, the German signaled that it was time to leave. As one of the kids brushed past us, Moss patted him on the shoulder and murmured, *"Buena Suerte,"* good luck. The boy looked pleased — there are, after all, a great many Colombians in Miami, but as yet very few Paraguayans — but, predictably, evinced no surprise whatsoever to find himself addressed in Spanish. Why should he have, since Spanish was in all likelihood the only language he had heard spoken during his stay? Shyly, he grinned his thanks. "If only," I thought, momentarily overcome by a rancorous envy at this easy sense of belonging, "I could have surprised him with a few words of Guarani." Instead, I wearily reeled in enough of my own Spanish to order another brandy. Or was it cognac?

Moss and the old man were busy evaluating Paraguay's chance that night. They were not, it appeared, exactly brilliant. At last Moss made our excuses and we walked out into the sharp late-afternoon sunlight. The buildings crazily mirrored one another's shapes, and, for a moment, I was seized by the fancy that these skyscrapers had metamorphosed into giant condors easing toward flight. I wasn't even daydreaming with any geographical accuracy. As any Hispanic Miamian could doubtless have informed me, there are no condors in Paraguay.

After leaving Moss at his car, I decided to walk back

to the hotel. In the side streets, gaggles of what travel agents call "downmarket" tourists clustered by the windows of the cut-rate electronics shops. Even when they pointed they seemed to be speaking Spanish. The rush hour was still a noise in the distance, an implication. Already the Anglos were going home and the Cuban middle class along with them. José Arenal had commented to me only half-jokingly that in downtown Miami, at five, all the Cuban office workers raced for their cars like frightened hares because "the blacks were coming." Oh America. It was almost as if metropolitan life had been reorganized into two shifts — one respectable, the second feral.

Rather than go directly up to my room, I decided to walk down to the hotel pool. Dusk teetered as if unwilling to fall, and the air, though not yet cool, was no longer so cloying and still. I sat on a granite parapet staring out into Biscayne Bay, as the pool boys rushed to and fro piling the deckchairs into odd mounds and ziggurats. In his novel *The Green Ray*, Victor Hugo wrote of a special greenish flash of light which, appearing at sunset, could impart wisdom. I didn't need wisdom, I thought sourly, I needed Captain Nemo to come rescue me. But eventually the sight of the speedboats cutting a few long, final figure-eights through the opalescent chop, the feel of the wind, almost ludicrously fresh even in the middle of downtown, the sight of the stars — in other words, all the postcard clichés of Miami — were infinitely calming. When I finally went up to my room, I ordered some food from room service, and, quite cheerfully, settled down to watch a soccer game.

From the opening kick, it was clear that the announcers on the Spanish International Network — a

Miami-based, at the time Mexican-owned broadcast group which is one of the three or four largest privately held television companies in Latin America — were directing their comments far more to their viewers in Mexico City or in Lima than to Cuban Miami or Mexican Houston. Cuban-American housewives might be addicted to Mexican soap operas like the divinely titled "The Rich Cry Too," but their husbands and sons were far more likely to watch the Miami Dolphins play football in the Orange Bowl. As far as sports were concerned, SIN's real audience lay to the south. Indeed, it occurred to me that one of the main points of holding a soccer game in Miami was that the city was probably the only neutral Hispanic venue anywhere in the Americas, and that this, along with the availability of reliable "First World" technology, was the attraction. To be sure, Miami could only look like Switzerland when viewed from the south, since, from the north, it looked like . . . Latin America.

In due course, Medellín won, 4-0, in the walkover everyone had predicted. I went to bed humming newly acquired bits of Colombia's tuneful national anthem (they had better composers than Paraguay, too) and chewing on the bizarre idea of Miami, that least Swiss of cities, as Latin America's Geneva.

9

IF THE ANIMALS had been let in on what God had confided to Noah about His upcoming aquatic spectacular, it is unlikely they would have consented to an immigration quota of one couple per species. People in Latin America are quite capable of seeing their situation realistically. After twenty years of insurgencies and counterinsurgencies, triple-digit inflations and the cruel, corrective austerities of Milton Friedman, demographic explosions, and ecological self-mutilations, even the most Pollyannaish among them had begun to despair. If anything, everyone told you, things would get worse. The lines of the Chilean poet, Nicanor Parra, summed up the apocalyptic, morbid despair of the Latin-American middle class by the end of the nineteen-seventies. In his poem "Modern Times," Parra wrote:

We're living through horrible times
It's impossible to say anything without contradicting
yourself
impossible to hold your tongue without being a pawn of
the Pentagon.
Everyone knows there's no other possible choice

all roads lead to Cuba
but the air is filthy
and breathing is a waste of time.
The enemy says
nations are to blame
as if nations were individuals.
Wretched clouds swirl around wretched volcanos
condemned ships undertake hopeless expeditions
wretched trees dissolve into wretched birds:
all contaminated from the start.

It was not only the middle class that, to borrow
another image of Parra's, seemed to have its whole
death in front of it. By the beginning of the nineteen-
eighties, rich and poor alike were gearing for departure. And there was nowhere else to go but to the
United States. Western Europe borders on the sea and
the Soviet Empire, and, in any event, its gates were
closing. The United States borders on the Third World,
the only developed country to do so. The Mexicans
were already arriving in the American Southwest. Now,
illegal immigrants began to have a second destination:
Miami. The slang for the jumping-off point into California was *el hueco* (Mexico); to this was added a new
code, *la isla*, the Bahamas.

Anglos confronted by the phenomenon of this new
migration tended, in Miami as elsewhere, to talk balefully of overcrowded lifeboats. The truth was starker.
"Miami," Frank Soler observed, "is Noah's Ark. It's
that simple." And it was clear that, to gain sanctuary
in Miami, the poorest refugees would go to any lengths.
If one compares the reports in the newspapers today
with those of five years ago, the only change seems
to be the immigrants' country of origin. The stories
of the Haitian boat people rarely rate more than a

mention, but both the *Miami Herald* and the more sensation-mongering *Miami News* are glutted with accounts of desperate people trying to make their way North — accounts which, as immigration policy has grown stricter and enforcement more effective, have appeared to grow almost exponentially more heart-rending, more pathetic.

There was the group of Dominican men who had tied a bunch of inner tubes together and floated in the Florida Strait for two weeks, bobbing north from Grand Bahama Island until, bloated with dehydration, they landed, the dead and the living, at the Pier House Hotel marina in downtown Key West — a place that draws in tourists from around the world. There was the Colombian teenager who tried to make his way to Miami cinched to the landing gear of a 747; he died. A group of Martiniquan women were transported in the hold of a freighter, nailed into wooden boxes among a load of green bananas; some of them lived.

I do not mean to give the impression that the voyage was somehow not worth the risk, that the behavior of the immigrants was pathological, an example of some extraordinary popular delusion, or, for that matter, some misapprehension about the United States. It wasn't. To be sure, the immigrants shared the same dreams of an America paved with gold which had fired their German, Italian, Polish, Irish, and Jewish predecessors a century before. But in the age of the jet airplane, immigrants move back and forth in a way unimaginable at the turn of the century. Most of those who come know what they are in for, but, as they are the first to tell you, even an America pockmarked with decay beats holy hell out of what life offers in the Caribbean and in Central America. "Back home," one Colombian said to me over a beer at a bar called "La Tranquera" — we could have been in Bogotá — "it is impossible to succeed." He used the Spanish verb *triunfar*, which also means "triumph." America is a last chance for that, too. "To triumph, then," I toasted him. Try to tell even an illegal who is down on his luck about poverty in America. The Colombians grimace; the Haitians giggle, if possible politely, out of earshot. And keep on trying to come.

Those who have succeeded receive an ambivalent welcome. In principle, Anglo Miami, despite an abiding, hardy strain of sympathy for the refugees, would rather they just stopped showing up. In practice, though, few middle-class Miamians could get by today without the illegal workers who take care of every dirty job technology has not itself done away with. Sometimes, the immigrants at the bottom — the Haitians, Salvadorans, Jamaicans, and Dominicans — seem to be regarded as labor-saving devices and little else. More frequently, their employers simply take them for granted much the way they take for granted the fact that coffee makers in Miami hotels have the instructions in Spanish or that in office buildings it often says *basura*, not "trash," by the dumpsters.

A few years ago, two cleaning ladies were denied jobs in an office tower because they did *not* speak Spanish. They sued, and, eventually, won. But the employer's fears were grounded in the reality of life in South Florida. Who ever heard of a cleaning lady who didn't speak Spanish in Miami? How was she going to communicate with the rest of the maintenance staff? How, indeed. This is not, of course, a situation peculiar to Dade County. Is there a white man or woman sweeping the streets, washing the dishes, or minding the children in any major city in the developed world anywhere between Slovenia and Hawaii? If so, she was not, I suspect, hired recently.

A whole industry has developed to allow English-speaking employers to communicate with their Spanish-speaking workers. There is a restaurant in South Miami that has Anglo waitresses, mostly college girls working part-time, and a kitchen staff without a green card among them. The owners have installed a computer. The waitresses punch in the customers' orders in English and the computer translates it into Spanish for the cooks. The arrangement seems to work perfectly, so well, in fact, that while the manager was happy enough to show the gadget off to me, he didn't quite see why I was making such a rapturous fuss about the whole thing.

Computers have not made their way into the home yet. However, many bookstores and a good many candy stores and card shops as well carry a line of books that have a similar purpose. The series is published in Contra Costa, California, but although, presumably as a result, the gardener's face on the cover of *Tell-a-Gardener* was distinctly Mexican, many an Anglo housewife I met in suburban South Dade admitted sheepishly to keeping a copy of the book "for reference," as the euphemism went, in the kitchen. I found their embarrassment honorable. Few Cubans had such scruples about being dependent on servants, while, it goes without saying, the nouveau riche Latin-Americans on Key Biscayne reveled in the fact with a positively Czarist enthusiasm.

In any case, these "Tell-a . . ." manuals are entirely matter-of-fact. There are lists of vocabulary, as well as sentences set out on separate sheets that instruct the gardener (or maid, or housekeeper, or nanny) to perform a task. There are also politely nagging formulations beginning "Did you?" One can either check the appropriate box and leave a copy of the instruction (each page is fully detachable from the booklet itself) on the kitchen counter or in the garden shed, or simply refer back for items of essential Spanish. No one in twenty-first-century America will be without one of these books.

What Miamians said about the illegal immigrants was somewhat contradictory. They responded to polls by supporting stricter immigration controls, applauding, to take only two instances, the building of the Krome detention center and the stationing of the Coast Guard cutter in the straits. Politicians who stressed the "menace" posed by illegal immigration were unlikely to suffer on election day, and, of course, the airwaves were full of bombast and invective. When pressed, however, in private, the tone shifted. Most people I talked to seemed to feel that, whatever they might wish would happen, there was really nothing much that could be done.

The animus of the Anglos remained far more fixed on Cubans who were perceived as competitors. There was hysteria there, all right, as there was about AIDS. Only, I felt, when the question of the illegal aliens brushed up against those deadlier issues did real hostility come into play. Thus, an Anglo Miami already up in arms over bilingualism received the influx from Central America which began in the wake of the Salvadoran Civil War almost as unfair reinforcements for the Cuban side. Similarly, the suggestion that Haitians were AIDS carriers did more to turn people against them in Miami than did any other single fact. Even today, there are rumors that the Center for Disease Control in Atlanta really took the Haitians off the AIDS list because of pressure by civil rights groups.

Even an issue as divisive as bilingualism or as terrifying as AIDS was not enough to excite Anglo Miami except intermittently. The countervailing pressures were, in any case, as strong if not stronger. Illegal immigrants are now not only an inextricable part of the economy of South Florida (particularly, as throughout the country as a whole, in the restaurant and hotel businesses), but also an inseparable element in the lives of so many middle-class people (particularly, for obvious reasons, those who have children and live in single-family homes). It is hard to imagine anyone becoming truly serious about expelling them, as, say, Nigeria did its Ghanaian guest-workers (there were a million of them; the army rounded them up and marched them to the border) in 1984, or even of offering them inducements to return home, as some European countries have tried to do in recent years. In Dade County, the cry is more a querulous "Enough" than a ruthless, patriarchal "No."

Books and Books is an admirable store in Coral Gables. I used to go there frequently during my stays in Miami, feeling a bit like a serviceman who after a long tour of duty gets weekend R and R in some longed-after fleshpot. I would dawdle in this haven for hours, staring covetously at the long, kempt shelves of poetry, fiction, and history. It was a place to decompress, to chat with the owner, Mitchell Kaplan, or just to avoid thinking about Miami. Kaplan does not, obviously, stock the "Tell-a . . ." series, which did not, as it turned out, mean that his customers didn't ask for it, or, more frequently, for somewhat tonier manuals for communicating with their "help." One could get blind-sided by these requests, as when a well-dressed man strolled in, asking for a book with which to teach a child to read the alphabet.

"What age, sir?" Mitchell asked him, reasonably enough.

The fellow blushed, replying, "Oh no, it's for our housekeeper. She's a Tamil, you see. The problem my wife and I have is that she doesn't know how to read our letters." Then, almost as an afterthought he added: "Their alphabet is different. It doesn't look anything like ours." Then, brightening, "Except the *d*."

In the Krome detention center for illegal aliens there are detainees from at least thirty-five countries. After the Haitians and the Colombians come the rest of Central America and the Caribbean basin. Recently, however, Immigration police have been catching more and more South Asian immigrants. They use the same route, setting forth from the Bahamas across the strait. How does one say *la isla* in Tamil or Tagalog, Vietnamese or Urdu? There are captains in Grand Cayman and Nassau who know the answer to that, hard-eyed men who know a smattering of every language the poor speak. If in Miami English is under siege, in Krome the place of Spanish itself is hardly so secure as most assume.

Different kinds of refugees (a polite way of saying refugees with differing amounts of cash and property) are, of course, afforded varying degrees of welcome. With bad grace, Miami shelters the West Indians and Central Americans. As the civic eye scans up from the bottom of the refugee pecking order, a smile begins to play at the corner of the civic mouth. Miamians may feel threatened by the tens of thousands of hardworking, largely lower-middle-class immigrants from Latin America who have installed themselves in a vast sprawl of tract housing on the western and southern edges of Dade County, but they respect them as well. For one thing, the new arrivals have caused a tremendous building boom, and Miami is simply not programmed to think unkindly of economic growth, whatever its social origin.

At first, these immigrants had lived in Miami proper, in those sections of Little Havana that had been vacated by the upward heave of Cuban-American prosperity. A Colombian bar like La Tranquera is located in the heart of Little Havana on a site which, only ten years ago, housed a Cuban restaurant. But Cuban-Americans remain attached to Little Havana, at least as a business center, and in any case the numbers of Latin-American immigrants soon became simply too great for any more people to be crammed into these progressively shabbier apartment complexes around the Orange Bowl. These, in any case, were becoming the territory of those Cubans without money, the *marielitos* — a group even a people as tough as the Colombians found daunting. Thus, to the already nearly indecipherable confusion of Dade County, with its twenty-seven distinct municipalities, was added a riotous addendum of unincorporated housing tracts — collectively known as townhouse and condominium "communities," and generically known as subdivisions.

The Cubans, already almost half the county (750,000 people) in absolute numbers, were, obviously, already in the suburbs. They were taking over politically. By

the end of 1985, Hialeah, no longer simply a sprin-
kling of houses around the celebrated racetrack, had
become overwhelmingly the blue-collar Cuban city,
and its mayor, Raúl Martinez, was in his third term.
Within a year, the county manager's job would go to
a Cuban, Sergio Pereira, and, finally, a Cuban, Xavier
Suárez, would become mayor of Miami in 1986.

Attention to these events tended to mask the movement of the other Latin-American groupings in Miami.
For example, the town of Sweetwater (the name, a
typical Florida boom concoction, makes one want to
look warily around for water moccasins) has, over the
course of the last five years, become largely a Nicaraguan enclave. Driving around Sweetwater, I was reminded of the fact that not only is it possible to live
in Miami without speaking any English, but that in
the southwestern parts of the city one rarely hears
any English spoken at all. In the local shopping center,
at the Shell station, in the fast-food outlets, I never
heard an English sentence unless I had instigated it.
Then people politely switched gears.

The signs were still bilingual, and were recognizable in the same way that the suburban sprawl was
recognizably American. But the use of English was
either haphazard (as if the person who had made the
sign didn't actually know what the words meant) or
seemed curiously antiquated and ceremonial like the
bits of Old French that are sprinkled through British
legal documents. As for the cultural cross-currents,
these could be astonishing. I saw a sign proclaiming,
"Authentic Nicaraguan and Italian Cuisine" and a
restaurant named All the Americas, which had a
clientele to match. What appeared to me at first as an
undifferentiated Hispanic mass turned out, under closer

inspection, to be an anthology of Spanish America, and I spent a number of evenings listening to Cuban friends ogle the waitresses and argue whether one was Honduran, or Costa Rican, or Colombian, or Mexican. Being second-generation Cubans, they didn't always guess right — a fact which embarrassed them and fascinated me. "You're halfway to becoming Anglos," I'd tease them.

Meanwhile, when I would tell my Anglo friends about this side of their own city I was constantly surprised both by their ignorance and by their indifference. Miami seemed unknown to Miamians. Yet it was there for all to see. In exile, a branch of the Somoza family has gone straight and now runs a very creditable steakhouse — one of the best in Dade County, in fact — in one of the Sweetwater malls. The restaurant is much favored by the faculty of adjacent Florida International University. But apart from giggling about the thought of the relatives of the bloodthirsty dictator serving steaks and lobsters, no one seemed very interested in this new world that was being born all around them. And yet to drive from the new brutalist buildings of the F.I.U. campus to the restaurant, one had to pass the huge sign erected by the town of Sweetwater, which monolingually wished visitors a hearty "*Bienvenidos.*"

It is a commonplace, this immigrant need to own a piece of property, to grab a stake, however small, in the new country. Even after twenty-six years, at a time when Cuban-Americans are more likely to be buying banks and shopping malls than downmarket condos, one still sees, throughout Little Havana, hand-lettered or cheaply printed cards offering real estate. "For Sale." *Se vende.* Usually, what is being offered is a half-acre in Hialeah, a share in a townhouse in West Miami, or a modest apartment in Miami Springs, listings no realtor could unload. But even on hot days in Miami, people stop to look at these neat little notices, savoring the idea of ownership even when they can't afford to buy — like black teenage lovers looking into a jewelry store window. *"Se vende,"* the signs say, twinkling out through the reinforced, bulletproof glass of the shop fronts.

If one starts driving west along Eighth Street in the flag-draped heart of Little Havana, the banks, *farmacías*, restaurants, and Mom-and-Pop convenience stores soon give way to subdivisions and the smell of swampwater. A four-lane city street turns into a six-lane suburban parkway, the Tamiami Trail. Follow it all the way and you find yourself passing the turnoff for Krome before, finally, butting into the Everglades. To your left, tract housing as far as you can see, and to your right, a bayou known as the Tamiami Canal — the "Boating Prohibited" signs spaced at regular intervals. This scenery is invariant, an unrelieved flatness tiring to the eye. And yet how cosy it must seem to the people who live in it; people who have fled those comely, baroque cities that the fine architects and military engineers of the Vice-Royalty of New Spain erected with such pomp; people who are the new Americans.

Soon billboard advertising begins to claim the motorist's attention. Uniformly in Spanish, these signs trumpet a seemingly inexhaustible array of subdivisions, all with fetching, reassuring names. To my jaundiced eye, by now accustomed to New York landlords charging four figures for a space that might have been used to house white-collar criminals in Scandinavia, the prices were startlingly low. Even by Miami

[117]

standards, the tracts were cheap, the mortgages generous. Curiously, the advertisers chose to retain English when describing particular conveniences in the individual houses. Gratefully, the eye encountered familiar words like *double-height ceilings*, *two-car garages*, *bidets* (a recent fad), or *central air-conditioning*; they were like old friends or schoolmates. But for the immigrant, there are the linguistic comforts of home, and the totemic reassurances of those bits of English.

For a time, before he moved back North to New Jersey, in flight from what he had come to think of as "that Cuban ghetto," Heberto Padilla lived in one of these Southwest Dade subdivisions. His own particular development, which lay a good hour from the center of Miami by car even in light traffic, was called Villa Venezia. "Hello, Addison Mizner," I thought, the first time Padilla took me there. And, sure enough, at the gate, there was the granite prow of a gondola pushing, crookedly tumescent, into the cloying, hibiscus-scented air. A teenager streaked by on a skateboard, crouched low. We parked. "Well," Padilla said, shrugging, as we walked toward the house, "you are in Venice. It's that simple."

Villa Venezia was surrounded by a dozen other developments, indistinguishable one from the other except by their lyrical monikers. There were names in Spanish: Lago Grande, which did border a lake, though not one made in nature; Costa del Sol was a good ten miles from the shores of Biscayne Bay and three thousand miles off course if you wanted to get technical; then there was El Paradiso, on which I will refrain from commenting except to note that it lies within spitting distance of the Hialeah Race Track. There were the usual Oak Groves, Bay Garden Manors, and

Palm Gardens. Then there were the moral equivalents of "continental cuisine," subdivisions with names which simply seemed peculiar or out of place: Kendall Royale, Tanglewood, and L'Hermitage. But no matter what the names, if one drove past the houses at dinnertime one would hear, even through rolled-up car windows, Spanish soap operas blaring out like air-raid warnings.

Southwest Miami is often a depressing place, an anthology of middle-class clichés — the bike on the lawn, Daddy coming home from a hard day at the *oficina*, Mom with her list of complaints, dinner smells. These values and styles never strayed far from being dubbed-in-Spanish versions of fifties sitcoms like "Father Knows Best" and "Leave It to Beaver." Excepting the faces of some of the old people (America, coming at the tail end of their lives, could not do much to alter their physiognomies) and the very young, there was little character. And yet, finally, aesthete that I am, I was still curiously undisturbed by this. I was no longer able to laugh at people whose ambitions had nothing to do with mine, who did not want interesting lives but had come in search of safe, prosperous ones. To bend a saying of Brecht's slightly, "First grub, then aesthetics." There were worse fates than to live in "plastic" environments; most, in fact.

I did not change my mind when, back in New York, I played host to the daughters of a rich Munich businessman. They had been in the city for two months and were living in a sixth-floor walk-up in a neighborhood which was dangerous even during the day. They told me that they found living there "really interesting," and asked me why I lived in "such a safe, boring part of town." I told them that if they stayed for a while they would see.

10

I WAS UNABLE to return to Miami for some time. In part, the reasons for this were practical: my life in New York grew suddenly, unexpectedly hectic — a morose thicket of obligations and deadlines. But, although I was loath to admit it, I was not in fact particularly eager to make another trip south. During my last visit, I had felt curiously aloof, as though I had already amassed — preposterous notion though it might be — more impressions of Miami than I could assimilate. Worse, I had started feeling that my ability to look at the city in an intelligent way was becoming progressively blunted, my impressions coarsened, by the very progress of my own increasing familiarity with the place. It was as if I were no longer alien enough; the omnivorous curiosity of the stranger was giving way to the frequent visitor's blank stare. Significantly, my note-taking grew more dilatory, and I had stopped paying much attention to the cabdrivers who ferried me around the city; they, like the landscape, had become part of the landscape. Moreover — a bad sign — I had taken to wearing that observation-suppressing machine, a Walkman, which I played at high volume as I sped between appointments.

In his wonderful book *Soft City*, the English writer Jonathan Raban distinguishes between the "soft city" of "illusion, myth, aspiration, and nightmare," and the "hard city" "one can locate on maps, in statistics, in monographs on urban sociology and demography and architecture." But without the energy to enchant or bewilder or mystify, Raban's soft city (the one the writer must find in order to write) is nothing more than a backdrop, a hazy outline of buildings and people one glimpses as one moves about on one's private business, and apprehends no more clearly than one does when staring down at a residential street through the window of a climbing airplane. Soon, I feared, I would take Miami so entirely for granted that whatever facility I had gained for describing it would disappear. It was, I suspected, only through the "hard city" — through lists and cold fact — that I would be able, paradoxically, to make Miami strange again, "soft" again.

From a friend in Coral Gables I obtained a copy of the Greater Miami telephone directory; it sat on my kitchen counter for weeks, like a rare orchid, and I would page through it most mornings, before going off to work. Divorced from their function, those two thick volumes became for me almost autonomic goads to reverie. With quickening excitement, I traced the columns of Hispanic surnames — "Miranda, Mario," "Miranda, Marisol," "Miranda, Marta." Other facts — Miami crime, Miami capitalism — seemed legible again as I paged through the business listings: "Mirrors; Wholesale and Manufacturers," "Missile and Rocket Components: Manufacturers," "Missing Persons Bureaus," "Missing Persons Traced; See Collection Agencies." The real life of Dade County was there at my fingertips, there in a harsh, icy language more arresting, in type, than those opaque snapshots my direct observations had become.

I read. There were the U.S. government health studies, stews of terrifying statistics about South Florida, which chronicled with what often seemed excessive thoroughness the relative incidence in the population of such divergent conditions as obesity (Jews, Cubans, and, for somewhat different reasons, blacks), malnutrition (blacks and Haitians), AIDS (gays, intravenous drug users, and, depending on the year the study had appeared and the scruples of the research team, Haitians), and skin cancer (all white people who appeared unshrouded at the local beaches were, it seemed, at risk). I found demographic projections that seemed to conclude that although Florida would likely be the third largest state in the union by the year 2000, there wouldn't be enough water pressure to power the jet of a single bidet south of Fort Lauderdale. And there were a pharaoh's tomb's worth of immigration reports. On that desperate subject, even the foundation studies were written in a style that would not have displeased the city editor of even the seamiest of Mr. Rupert Murdoch's pestilential tabloids. One book was called *Clamor at the Gates*. They might as well have used the title "Disgusting Colored Hordes at the Door" and have done with it.

Most evenings, I would return home in darkling, wintry New York to the tropical gouaches of days-old Miami newspapers. The tales they had to tell seemed less like the tragedies they overwhelmingly were than like melodramas in which the blood was ketchup and the tears the dubious exertion of method acting. Even in one's own native place, after all, it is hard not to find the events of the day as reported on television and in the papers to be anything but faintly unreal —

even at their grisliest or most heartbreaking. As for real horror or pity, there is more of that in the sight of a beggar vomiting at the curb than in all the TV accounts of rape and murder put together. That being said, to watch the nightly news anywhere in America is, by now, largely an act of voyeurism — rec-room pornography. How can it be otherwise in a country whose 9,800 civilian deaths by gunfire comprise nine out of ten such casualties worldwide?

In New York, at a distance of eleven hundred miles, the images of Miami as filtered through its newspapers seemed the baldest works of fiction, or, more precisely, like particularly riveting soap operas. Would the West Kendall rapist ever get caught? (He did.) Would Cuban mayoral candidate Raúl Masvidal (whose detractors called him *más dinero*, more money) gain the endorsement of the liberal *Miami News*? (He did.) Would Commissioner Joe Carrollo accept Bay of Pigs veteran/businessman Jorge Mas Canosa's challenge to a duel over the Watson Island development scandal? (The more Americanized Carrollo scoffed at the idea.) And what other improprieties would Judge Alcee Hasting, Jr., be accused of committing from the privileged perch of his high office? (The number grew.) These newspaper accounts of Miami conformed absolutely to the image of a city that was the second coming of the Chicago of Al Capone. But while Chicago in the nineteen-twenties was still the home of modern "skyscraper" architecture, and of the poet Carl Sandburg as well, no such counterbalancing cultural distinction could console the citizens of Miami.

This is not to say that all South Florida's evocations of itself were apocalyptic. To the contrary, most were remorselessly self-promoting. I pored over such exercises in boosterism as the glossy *South Florida*, with

[123]

its ever more florid accounts of ever more French restaurants springing up in North Miami Beach; the high-minded *Caribbean Review*, which carried accounts of Afro-Cuban culture so invidiously respectful that even a black nationalist would have been bored stiff; *Miami Mensual*, Frank Soler's magazine for the so-called YUCCAS — young, up-and-coming Cuban-Americans; and even the endlessly diverting *Proyecto*, the Spanish-language organ of the Latin American Builders Association of Dade County.

In this exalted mood, Miami, which was, after all, my private obsession, seemed ubiquitous. I could not even cross a street in New York without overhearing something or seeing something that evoked the place. On the wall of the celebrated National Guard Armory in New York, where, seventy-four years ago, European modernist art was first shown in America, a graffito muttered illiterately about "unemployed victoms of emigration." In a coffee shop near my office, I heard a rather frayed, elderly woman pull herself together before walking out into the chilly street and wonder whether it wasn't time to pack up and join her sister on Miami Beach. At a dinner party given by some friends whose interest in Miami or in Cuba was, as far as I knew, nonexistent, I was astonished to find, upon ducking into the bedroom to make a phone call, a book on the Bay of Pigs grinning up at me from the nightstand. As the party carried on in the next room, I read the last lines of this book (written in 1963):

> It is seven years since another small band of freedom fighters was crushed and the lights went out in Hungary. Today, in their moments of despair and bitterness, the Cuban exiles often refer to Hungary. They do not know what their future holds, but they are

determined that they are not going to live a lifetime in exile, in the manner of the White Russians and the Hungarians. Each is waiting to return to Cuba.

Who could have imagined how the very meaning of exile itself would be transformed over the following twenty years so that, in 1986, Rafael Soriano, perhaps the best twentieth-century Cuban painter after Wilfredo Lam, could gesture around his modest Miami studio and declare: "I like Miami, because there is no Cuba anymore. This is the only place I belong to." Or that the Cuban writer Guillermo Cabrera Infante could address a largely Cuban-American audience in Miami and remark, with perfect irony and perfect justice, "There is no success like exile."

The special advertising supplement entitled "The Cuban Success: A Realization of the American Dream" arrived discreetly, wrapped in the voluminous folds of the Sunday edition of the *New York Times* like a derringer in a billowing skirt. "What," the introductory paragraph demanded, "do the chief executive officer of Coca-Cola, Nancy Reagan's haute couture designer, a world champion runner, and America's top ballet dancer, have in common?" The punchline was, of course, that "they are all Cuban-Americans — products of the mass of humanity that began pouring into the United States in overwhelming numbers after the Castro regime took control of Cuba in 1959." The anonymous authors (advertising copywriters, from the hurly-burly of their prose) went on to describe how the Cuban-American community had overcome both "adversity" (that is, arriving penniless in the United States) and "fear" (that is, the overwhelming, rabid hostility of the English-speaking citizens of South

Florida), but had turned both of these "events" into something Ronald Reagan, the Burbank freedom fighter himself, might have described as swell. After twenty-six years, the verdict was in: Cubans in America had succeeded beyond their own and everyone else's wildest expectations. In case there were any doubters, here, in the Sunday *New York Times*, the national newspaper of record, was the documentation to prove it. So it turned out to be a plug for Cuban businessmen paid for by Cuban businessmen. Isn't that the way George Merrick had sold Coral Gables?

The opening remarks of the supplement ended with a bit of bravado. Cubans, it was asserted, had turned their misfortunes into such a good thing that they even had reason to be grateful for having been thrown unceremoniously into exile. They could even tartly thumb their collective nose at Castro, saying *Gracias, Fidel*. Perhaps the laughter was grim, but it was still laughter. Reading "The Cuban Success," I was reminded of the Miami joke about Cuba. Cuba, the story goes, is a vast country. The island is in the Caribbean, the government is in Moscow, the army is in Africa, and the people all live in Miami.

The brochure itself was constructed like a corporation's testimonial dinner. After the self-congratulatory opening remarks came a compendium of further congratulatory remarks, "quotes from other [i.e., Anglo] Americans." The Americans in question turned out to be none other than the President of the United States, the governors of Florida, New Jersey, and Puerto Rico, the mayor of New York City, and both Florida senators. Their remarks fell mostly into the "came with only the shirts on your backs, now you run the joint" school of heartfelt accolading, and carried the same conviction that movie stars bring to shilling for

the auto companies. There was, of course, considerable truth to the notion that Cuban-Americans had
been by far the most successful of all recent immigrant groups. But, reading between the lines, all these
neoconservative love songs to the zesty, bilingual en-
trepreneurship of Cuban Miami seemed, implicitly at
least, to admit the dispiriting truth that most other
recent immigrants to America were not faring particularly well. Not that any of this niggling worry made
any difference to the sponsors of the ad. They were
too busy patting themselves on their *guayabera*-clad
backs.

Usually, advertising supplements laid out like "The
Cuban Success" are used by smallish Third World
countries to flog themselves to potential investors,
soothe their creditors, and inveigle those elusive tourists. The drill is familiar: "Under the leadership of his
nattiness . . . , the Republic of Blank has made enormous strides toward . . ." Then the brochure usually
gets down to talking about the limitlessness of its
potash reserves and the pleasures of its beaches. In
contrast, "The Cuban Success" was the first example
of an ethnic group within the American polity trying
this approach. There had never, after all, been advertising supplements trumpeting "The Jewish Triumph"
or "The Splendid Slavs." But then, those groups established themselves in America before the advent of
that sea change known as advertising, into which,
rather like B.C. and A.D., American history can be
divided.

It is, of course, a commonplace that in modern
America everyone wants to be famous — and quickly,
if you please. Amongst the older, better established
ethnic groups, this desire is largely entertained by
individuals. But for as cohesive a group as Cuban-

Americans, the idea of some kind of collective celebrity — rather like a rock star with a million glitter-flecked heads — was not only natural; it was bound to be irresistible. At the same time, while "The Cuban Success" was in no way obviously defensive (it contained none of the pathetic assertiveness that seems to inform the morale-boosting slogans like "Black is beautiful," and their white-ethnic spin-offs like "I'm proud to be Polish," that can be seen on auto bumper stickers, T-shirts, and decals all over working-class America), the brochure did speak to considerable insecurity among Cuban-Americans. They did, indeed, protest too much. It was significant that it wasn't enough somehow for the Cubans of South Florida simply to have their success; everyone else had to see and approve if it were, ultimately, to be real. This need for Anglo sanction is an old thread in Cuban history, and constitutes, curiously enough, one of the links between the pre-1959 past in Havana and the present in South Florida. In Miami today, people use the same epithet that used to be current on the island in the days of Batista. *Plattista* derives from the Platt Amendment of 1901 that all but annexed Cuba to the United States in the wake of the Spanish-American War; and the prudent course is to be sure of one's company before using it heedlessly in Little Havana.

This *plattista* aura gave "The Cuban Success" a bizarre quality of triumphalism that was, simultaneously, supine. Still, whatever the felt need for President Reagan's goofy benediction (the appeal of which, in fairness, derived from the office, not the man), it was clear that Cuban-Americans were themselves quite overwhelmed by what they had accomplished during their first twenty-six years in the United States. This mixture of jubilation and disbelief is, moreover, one of the first things that the visitor notices in Cuban Miami, where it is all but impossible to walk into the office of any person of substance without encountering, on every available bit of wall space and shelving, a riot of diplomas, testimonials, certificates of civic achievement, service club awards, as well as photographs of one's host posed not only with the famous but with anyone with even the remotest claim to celebrity. These offices are not typical, I think, of any other group in America generally except, significantly enough, those of politicians and police officials, where it is of course quite normal to encounter this mixture of unslakable self-adulation and tremulous insecurity.

The point was driven home to me when, in the space of twenty-four hours, I visited the house of a Cuban film-producer in Miami and the apartment he maintained in Manhattan. In the latter, the walls were all postmodern chastity, bare surfaces enlivened only by the occasional print or drawing; but in Miami, my friend had hung not only the minor awards his films had received, but even the certificates of participation doled out by obscure Latin-American film festivals. Like Jimmy Cagney in *White Heat*, Miami seems to be forever shouting "Top of the world, Ma," but, unlike the gangster Cagney played, cocking an ear for Ma's reply.

As to the question of which world the authors of "The Cuban Success" had in mind, there could be little doubt. For all its lip service to other spheres of activity, the brochure was in fact concerned with little besides business. Indeed, the naïveté of the supplement on cultural matters in particular was evidenced by the naming of the excellent Cuban-American ballet dancer, Fernando Bujones, as "the world's best ballet dancer"; this in the age of the balletic supremacy of that other refugee from the Evil Empire, Mikhail Baryshnikov. The decision to elevate Bujones was very much in keeping with both Cuban braggadocio and Florida hype, almost as if reputation in dance were like an athletic event in which there was a winner and a bunch of insignificant also-rans. In Cuban Miami, of course, all professions are inferior to business and the bias of the brochure was only an extension of this pervasive viewpoint.

Not that "The Cuban Success" was in any way trying to conceal these biases; if anything, the reverse was the case. Indeed, before proceeding to "profile" — in terms that would have made even a corporate public relations officer think twice — the two dozen "representative" Cuban success stories whose uniformly plump faces and upper torsos adorned the cover, there was another preface, this time baldly titled "Cubans Mean Business." "When Calvin Coolidge declared," it began, "that the business of America is business, he probably never imagined that decades later a group of exiled Cubans would prove just how right he was." Perhaps?

The businessmen and -women (a revealing, immigrant touch, since it need hardly be added that Cuban Miami is not exactly a hotbed of feminism) in question ranged from rather important figures in regional banking, real estate, and construction engineering to a gaggle of far more modest, parochially South Florida success stories. The Dade County skew was unmistakable. To be sure, the supplement gamely tried to present the Cuban-American success as a nationwide phenomenon. But when push came to shove, it was the Cuban triumph in Miami that was being feted. There were "500-700 [Cuban-American] millionaires in the United States," the authors noted, adding with disingenuous surprise that "most of [them] reside in the Miami-Dade County area."

But whether rich or (as rich people like to say when they feel too much is being asked of them) simply well fixed, each profile was a love song to Cuban-American entrepreneurial drive, a paean of praise to the beneficent tides of capitalism, and, one felt, an almost Afro-Cuban mystical rite, an incantation against the return of bad times. "He became fascinated by real estate," one typical entry crooned, "saying 'I have this belief that if you have something to sell, you won't starve.' " It need scarcely be added that it was precisely this "belief" which had made Floridians rich since the days of George Merrick, and Americans since the days of P. T. Barnum. It is the credo of the salesman and the huckster.

Cuban culture is one in which self-promotion is one of the primary skills. Throughout the Caribbean Cubans have the reputation of being the preeminent snake oil salesmen. In Puerto Rico, Cubans are usually described as *listo*, a slang word whose rough English equivalent is "too clever by half." There is even a rather sick joke about a car crash, also from Puerto Rico. One foggy day in the mountains, the state police come on a three-car collision in which people have obviously been killed. But there are no bodies. A hundred yards down the road sits an old *jíbaro*, a peasant, puffing contentedly on his pipe. The cops drive up to him and ask what happened. "There was a crash, everyone was dead, I buried them," answers the old man simply. The cops are beside themselves. "What do you mean you buried them? You're supposed to call us," they wail. The old man is furious.

"They were dead, I tell you," he shouts; "in the first car they were decapitated, in the second crushed to death." "And the third car?" the police inquire. "Oh," the old man shrugs, "the third car was full of Cubans and they said they were alive, but you know Cubans."

In fact, Cubans in Miami tell similar anecdotes about themselves. Recently a Cuban friend was crowing to me about how well a mutual acquaintance was doing in his business. "He's the fourth biggest Hispanic film distributor in the country," the fellow said. Later that day, the success in question happened to call. I congratulated him. "Who told you I was fourth?" he asked sharply. I said a name. "Great!" he exclaimed. "I just told him that the other day and already he's spreading it around." *Listo*, indeed.

Alongside this exuberant flimflammery comes the more innocent pride in the achievement of prosperity. In another entry in "The Cuban Success," Mirta de Perales, the owner of what was rather mysteriously billed as "the first line of Hispanic cosmetics in the United States" (as if Hispanics were a race and not a linguistic group comprising a number of races), said of herself, in the third person singular, no less, that "when Mirta de Perales was ten years old she didn't even own a pair of shoes, and now, years later, she's been to the White House twice to be congratulated by two different presidents." The rather hard-bitten self-aggrandizement was immediately followed by a touching, wistful, intensely *plattista* conclusion. "Isn't it amazing," Mirta de Perales wondered.

Despite all the adornments of success, despite the "American Club," the Rotary clubs, the Kiwanis memberships, the civic good deeds, despite real estate and every other form of material success, the Cuban-American community is indeed wont to sigh with amazement and even some small discomfort at what it has achieved in America over the last twenty-seven years. One manifestation of this is a curious, persistent refusal to accept the fact that they are in South Florida to stay. In private, many utterly nonpolitical people will insist that, despite Cuban political and economic power in Dade County, they are not immigrants but exiles and that the final question of their status awaits a resolution that can come only after the death of Fidel Castro. This event, they assert with confidence, will make it possible for Cuban Miami to choose either Cuba or the United States. Until then, Cuban Miami is in the curious position of Cargo cultists who have struck oil. They are awash in material prosperity, but still, at least in their hearts, sneak off to worship the rusting hulk of a DC-3 that may still carry them back to the island.

The fantasy of return coexists with a desperate desire to belong, to make it in America, and the fizzy combination does much to account for the particular brashness, even the vulgarity of Cuban Miami. Immigrants, after all, are rarely well mannered once they have their foot in the door. Hungry for material things, hungry for recognition, they tend to show off. It isn't only cocaine dealers in Miami who are given to platinum Longines watches and heavy gold identification bracelets; everyone seems to have them. "Don't be too quick to make fun of the guy with three Cadillacs in his garage," Frank Soler admonished me; "he probably didn't even have a bicycle back home in Oriente." As with any group of poor people who have suddenly landed up prosperous, no amount of expensive new possessions can entirely make up for the wants of childhood. Indeed, it is really only the American (or at least Americanized) children of these bustling, voluble, self-made Cuban businessmen who seem comfortable lounging on the squeaky-clean couches and amidst the welter of electronic gizmos. To look into the eyes of the parents is to see, like a primitive special effect from a silent movie, the old shack outlined against the sleek silhouette of the Southwest Miami split-level, the creaky bicycle hovering before the electronic door of a three-car garage. Even in an advertising supplement like "The Cuban Success," this subtext was not hard to discern.

It was equipped with a copy of "The Cuban Success" that, a few weeks later, I ventured south again. The sleek New York businessmen striding athletically through midtown Manhattan contrasted oddly with those chubby faces on the brochure cover — emblems of Cuban Miami's premodern association of girth and prosperity. Boarding the flight at La Guardia Airport, I felt the Spanish language enveloped me like a benevolent uncle. Holidaymakers chatted, in English, about the good weather that awaited them in South Florida, while another family spoke exuberantly, in Spanish, about going home. In the seat pocket in front of me, someone had left a brochure, "Greater Miami and the Beaches," put out by the Greater Miami Tourism Council. A positively Visigothic platinum blonde in a slinky evening dress hovered, like an erotic dirigible, over a photograph of Miami Beach's Art Deco district. Inside the booklet, I couldn't find a single Spanish name. There was, however, a message announcing that the Miami Tourism Council would "like you to see Miami the way we see Miami." I wanted to say the same thing to them.

ON THE FLIGHT down to Miami, I had found myself seated next to a man whose concentration on the legal brief he had been examining did not survive the spell of sick-making turbulence we encountered over Chesapeake Bay. Unable to procure himself a drink (for the good and sufficient reason that it was nine-thirty in the morning: even Eastern Airlines' permissiveness has its limits), the man decided to make do with my company. Half swiveling around toward me in his seat, he gave me his best "ladies and gentlemen of the jury" cough, and, skipping right past the social niceties, began hectoringly to tell me the story of why he was going to Miami, beginning in the middle.

"My client — I can't tell you his name, that's privileged — had a wiretap put on him by those clowns in the U.S. Attorney's Office for South Florida. He's a lawyer, not that he defends dopers. He's not one of those gold Rolex lawyers, strictly corporate, but the Feds were convinced he was dirty and they thought they could nail him by bugging his office."

I scanned the rows behind. Like cops, there's never

a coke dealer around when you need one. Inexorably, the man continued.

"Those jerks actually wound up taping a confidential conversation with a client. Can you believe it — a privileged conversation?"

In such situations, what I mean to say is "I couldn't care less, get lost," while, invariably, what I actually say is "Oh, really," while flashing a wide, craven smile.

"Anyway," he continued, "I've got them cold. The only trouble is that all this means that I have to spend more time in Miami, and I hate Miami."

"You don't like Miami?" I inquired innocently. Heaven comes to those who wait.

"Like it," he sputtered. "I just despise the town. It's become a foreign city, nothing to do with America anymore. They should just deed it over to those Cubans."

And again he repeated, "It's not like America anymore." Neither is America.

The lawyer's withering dislike for Miami, based as it was on the conviction that at some point in the last twenty years it had stopped being an American city, was the rule rather than the exception among visitors to the city and Anglo residents alike. During the first few days I spent in Miami after my self-imposed months-long absence, I was struck even more forcefully than I had been in past trips by the distance between Cuban and Anglo Miami. It was not, in contrast to the other heavily Hispanic cities of the American Sunbelt, principally a matter of appearances, racial or otherwise. Indeed, outside the ever quainter-seeming purlieus of Little Havana (more and more transformed, in the nineteen-eighties, into a kind of theme park of the Cuban diaspora — "exileland"), middle-class Cubans and Anglos were hard to separate visually. For all the vaunted differences between them, they tended to drive the same makes of cars, live in similarly constructed subdivisions, and, among the whites who made up the bulk of the population, had even come to resemble one another physically. As for that hit soap opera known as the bilingualism crisis, that too was being worked out among the young under the Golden Arches of the local McDonald's, even if their parents refused to believe it.

The paradox was that in a community that in many ways had far more in common than, say, whites and the new immigrants from Hong Kong did in San Francisco or Seattle, the sense of alienation between the two groups persisted, bitterer than ever. Graver even than this hostility was the radical bifurcation between the two communities as a whole. Sometimes, as I shuttled between the Anglo and Cuban parts of Miami, I had the impression that only an outsider could comfortably have friends in both worlds. It was as if the laws of physics had somehow been altered so that the shared physical space of Miami had become, imaginatively at least, two superimposed territories — one Anglo, the other Cuban. Though they pined for home, the Cubans exuded a sense of well-being, of place. The Anglos, in contrast, seemed more and more to feel their city as an endangered species, in constant danger of being devoured by its Cuban roommate. Their alarm was not wholly unjustified.

Anglo Miami is a resort town somewhat past its prime which is now well on its way to recovering nicely into an important American provincial capital. Old-time Miamians, though they bemoan the passing of the resort, are more and more dependent economically on the business center. Indeed, the focus of the city's economic power has moved, over the course of the last two or even three decades, from Miami Beach and adjacent resort areas like Key Biscayne to the city of Miami itself, to Coral Gables, where many of the international banks are quartered, and to the port of Miami, which — assuming one combines the tonnage figures for cargo and passenger shipping — is now the largest in the United States. One by-product of this change can be observed in the fact that twenty years ago when a Miamian talked about Miami he might have been referring to any place from North Miami Beach to Coral Gables. Outsiders, of course, almost invariably meant Miami Beach when they said Miami. Today, the city itself is no longer a trailer hitched to the beach and the subtleties of municipal nomenclature suddenly have meaning. Until recently, the job of mayor of Miami — in contrast to that of the county and city managers — paid a paltry six thousand dollars a year, a throwback to the time when the office was a not very onerous part-time job. Now it is about to be properly salaried (although a Cuban friend, when I raised the point with him, pretended to have misunderstood me and blustered: "Only six thousand? Why I know lots of guys who would pay at least a quarter of a million for the job"). Like it or not, Miami is growing up.

Much of the change in Miami has, of course, more to do with the general transformation of the American economy (from heavy industry to service jobs, from the assembly line to computer terminal, from East-West to North-South). To some extent, they would have affected South Florida whether Fidel Castro had come down from the Sierra Maestra or not. However, as some less well mannered Cubans have a certain fondness for pointing out, without Cuban moxie it is hard to imagine that Miami would have become anything like the boomtown it is today. There is a rather loony Cuban politico in Miami called Estrella, who likes to go on television and in Spanish (he is always refusing to speak English because of some imagined slight or other) taunt Anglo Miamians by asserting that, before the Cubans arrived, the town was of no significance. Even more mainstream types gleefully point out that when the major Cuban businessmen left Havana they took with them only about twenty million dollars in capital. "It doesn't sound like very much now," a Cuban financier told the Cuban-American sociologist José Llanes, "but in 1959, twenty million dollars could buy you downtown Miami if you wanted it, which no one did back then." In private, even younger Cuban-Americans are dismissive about Anglo Miami. If they want Anglo, they go to New York. And Anglo Miamians know there is something to all this, that they have these odious Cubans to thank for much of their prosperity. So the city stews in its own resentment.

That being said, between the port, the banking and real estate businesses, the airport, and such huge corporate headquarters as the Burger King fast-food chain, the economic outlook for Miami is a good deal brighter than it is in many other parts of the country. It is unlikely, for example, that Miami is susceptible to the same kinds of dislocations as such energy-producing states as Texas and Louisiana; the Miami economy is already too diversified for that. On the cultural side there is also cause for optimism, particularly if the wealth created by these largely licit enterprises makes its hasty American way from being new money to being old money — that is, money with pretensions to virtue. Already, the Miami Opera is quite good, as is the fledgling ballet company started by Edward Villela, considered to have been the greatest male dancer in the history of the New York City Ballet. The Coconut Grove Playhouse, where *Waiting for Godot* had its American premiere in 1956, is going strong under its new director, Arnold Mittelman. While there is as yet no art museum in the proper sense (mainstream Miami museums are, for the most part, either tiny collections or exhibition spaces that mount those shows on tour throughout the country), there are more than enough important collectors in Dade County for it to seem a safe bet that sooner or later (probably later) a good museum building will be commissioned and a proper collection given a permanent home. In symphonic music, there are several orchestral groups as well as the altogether first-rate concert series organized, almost single-handedly, by an admirable woman called Judy Drucker. In any case, classical music in America is, more and more, an affair of galas and single performances.

But all of this is really to say nothing more than that if everybody really puts their backs into the effort, the city of Miami will wind up being economically more or less on the level of San Diego, while culturally it will be able to boast about the same number of cultural appurtenances as, say, Cleveland or Detroit. In the arts particularly, the talented young Anglos — the photographers, dancers, choreographers, painters, and poets — will still live in Miami with one eye cocked toward New York or Los Angeles, and, metaphorically at least, with their bags packed. For all the gale-force talk circulating in South Florida about how Miami will soon be the new Athens, or is becoming the next New York or L.A. (talk which, it need hardly be added, has accompanied the city from its inception), Miamians will, if rudely pressed, admit that their prospects are considerably more modest.

One can scarcely blame people in Miami Beach or Coral Gables for not liking to hear that things could hardly be otherwise in their little burg. Buddhistic acceptance comes rather easier to the visitor than to the resident. And yet, as Jack Webb liked to say on the TV series "Dragnet," those are "just the facts, ma'am." Miami was declining precipitously as a resort long before the Cubans made their presence so ostentatiously unavoidable. Even the rise of the cruise ship business is itself directly connected with the growing preference, among Northern holidaymakers, for the beaches and casinos of the Caribbean to the Art Deco of Miami Beach. But even this is more or less a side issue. Miamians, I suspect, would have found a way to get used to most of the changes which have come to their city, even those that grieve them, were it not for the constant reminder that for their Cuban neighbors Miami may not be Havana but it's the next best thing. In fact, it is precisely the degree to which Cubans feel at home in Miami that makes the Anglos disenfranchised, homeless.

Anglo Miamians do not, after all, obsessionally discuss the doings of the Haitian and Central American refugees who have poured into the city over the past decade. These people may be viewed as intruders, but, unlike the Cubans, they are not thought to have arrogated the town to themselves. To be sure, like all white people in America, Anglo Miamians know that faint apocalyptic twitch, that ticcky intimation of a future in which the United States will be a heavily non-white nation. Demographers have confidently forecast, in stories which I saw widely featured in the South Florida papers, that in less than a hundred years whites will make up less than fifty percent of the country. Indeed, to have this in your head, to walk through American streets on which every race is present, and then, late at night, to switch on the television to the all-Caucasian certainties of nineteen-fifties sitcoms — the Los Angeles of "Dragnet," a city without Mexicans, the Irish and Italian Brooklyn of Jackie Gleason's "The Honeymooners" — is to feel hard how history has so recently gone into fast forward. But this is the stuff of unhappy dreams, an intimation, perhaps, at its most extreme, not only of personal but of racial mortality.

Race, of course, is the great American subject, the subtext of the country's passions and its politics, the hidden, yawning fault line in its discourse. However, that is another subject. In the most immediate political sense, these new colored populations making their way into America's future have remained astoundingly quiescent. Even blacks, the oldest, most sinned-against of these peoples, don't vote proportionally to their numbers. The blacks seem almost on the sidelines now. Americans have, in the twentieth century, begun to confront the grim questions of black-white relations (think of the fact that the army was desegregated only forty years ago, the schools less than thirty), but the questions about white America's relation to the Third World will probably be postponed for quite a while to come. In all events, most whites who are alive today will not live to see much of this new, fully multiracial anthology the United States is bound to become, though, to be sure, their grand-children will. Only cramped fanatics think so far ahead.

The Cuban presence in South Florida is, for the Anglo population, something entirely different. Though it is certainly given additional weight by the advent, in the American imagination and on America's shores, of the mestizo peoples to the South — and how priv-ileged it will be to be a white Hispanic in the twenty-first century: the best of both destinies — the story of Cuban Miami not only has transformed South Florida but, as everything from "Miami Vice" to a feature on a Boston news show called "The Idea of Miami" showed, gained a remarkable purchase on the nation's imagination as well. Somehow, intuitively, Americans felt Miami was the future, even if, on the streets of Little Havana, I had a hard time under-standing quite how this future was different from the present.

The poor tend to wait a generation before kicking up their civic heels; middle-class immigrants like the Cubans are hardly so patient, particularly when the place they have migrated from is less than a hundred miles away. In the twenty-seven years they have been in Dade County, the Cuban population has succeeded in taking over, probably for generations to come, both the political and what must, for lack of a better word, be called the "atmospheric" control of the city of Miami. Obviously, they had been able to accomplish this precisely because of the peculiar way in which Miami had always been up for grabs (a phrase that quite correctly had served as the title for a good book on Florida by the Miami journalist John Rothchild).

You can't keep on repeating for half a century, "Miami the Magic City," "Miami the place that will be anything you want it to be," and then, when a couple of hundred thousand clever driven immigrants arrive with their work ethic and their memories, say, "Sorry, Cubans, Miami will always remain what it was twenty years ago when *we* first moved here." Perhaps that might work in the real Venice or Salamanca; it won't wash in South Florida.

When the Cuban refugees first began arriving in South Florida, they carried with them, all but intact, the ashes of bourgeois Havana. They no more meant to move into an alien environment than a person who transports his house trailer across a county line means to live in a different house. The immigration authorities in the early nineteen-sixties did not understand this. Indeed, for a while it was made more difficult for Cubans to live in Miami than in any other part of the United States. The city attempted not to issue business licenses anywhere north of Eighth Street to people who did not speak English (this is why Little Havana is in Southwest Miami and also why older Cubans still think of Flagler Street, the thoroughfare a few blocks north of the Calle Ocho, as "the Anglo street"). The federal authorities undertook a massive effort to relocate the Cuban refugees in New York and New Jersey. Over a hundred thousand were moved, well over half returned to Dade County. Miami was a way of being close to Cuba, of maintaining the possibility of returning, and most of all, of keeping "Cubanness" alive. The refugees stayed in Miami. And, like a wriggling fish, the city jumped out of those Anglo hands that had been trying to net it, back into the Caribbean waters in which it had been swimming all along. It is worth noting in passing that maps of the continental United States have to be tinkered with in order to fit South Florida into the frame, whereas maps of the Caribbean can't even be drawn properly without including it.

This, rather than racism or xenophobia, is what lies at the heart of the hysterical, desperate dislike that so many Anglos — visitors and residents alike — feel when confronted by the new state of play in Miami. Repeatedly, I encountered Miamians whose impeccably tolerant views of Haitian, Honduran, or Southeast Asian refugees in Dade County were utterly at odds with their resolute hostility toward all things Cuban. Simple sympathy for the underdog was insufficient to account for it, and I puzzled over these rhapsodic accounts of the Haitians' gentleness and nobility of spirit, the Hondurans' ebullience, or the spirit of enterprise exhibited by the Vietnamese boat people, until I realized that these accolades were in reality a masked way of damning the Cubans.

Even the most interesting people I met in Anglo Miami seemed peculiarly hard on the Cubans. At Books and Books in Coral Gables, I met a young photographer named Gary Monroe. Raised on Miami Beach, Monroe had, for the last decade, been documenting the fast-disappearing life of the Orthodox Jewish retirees of South Miami Beach in a series of heartbreaking, painfully observant black and white images reminiscent of the work of Roman Vishniac. Recently, Monroe told me, he had become interested in the Haitians. "I went to photograph the Haitian men being held in detention at Krome," he recounted enthusiastically, as we leafed through one of his portfolios. "They had been put in showers for delousing —

something which as a Jew made me shiver — and I got in there with them. I must have been less than a foot away as I took these pictures." He paused. "You know, they couldn't have been nicer or more cooperative. Afterwards, one of the guards told me that if it had been Cubans I'd been photographing they probably would have tried to kill me."

Monroe is a decent, scrupulous man. But as he spoke it never seemed to occur to him — and this was more than simply the occupational callousing of the photographer's trade — that the response which he imputed to the *marielitos* who had been held in Krome the year before was not only understandable but might, perhaps, be more human, more dignified, than the Haitians' docile, stuporous acquiescence.

This harsh double standard masquerading as high-mindedness was everywhere. Even when the habits at issue were shared by Cubans and Haitians alike, the reaction among the Anglos was predictably different. Voodoo, to take an extreme example, was a custom which, when practiced by the Haitians, was only mildly derided (and, indeed, often described as a charming foible). When practiced by Cubans, however, Santería became a cause for hand-wringing lamentations about the coming of the barbarians to Dade County. "You find goats' heads in their [i.e., Cubans'] refrigerators," complained a secretary I met at a party given by a group of West Kendall obstetricians. The Cubans' eating habits were the least of it. More gravely, they were held to have transformed South Florida from a forward-looking, politically liberal place, to the most politically reactionary community anywhere in America.

"They're taking away our political liberties," an art

dealer in North Miami assured me. She was referring to the Dolores Prida case. Dolores Prida is a left-leaning Cuban-American playwright, who, sensibly enough, lives in New York. An intrepid Miami theatre producer decided to include something by Prida in a Cuban festival in Miami. The play created a firestorm. There were anonymous bomb threats, and, more importantly perhaps, the whole spectrum of Cuban Miami, from right to right, denounced Prida and the festival organizers. The play was hastily withdrawn.

The rhetoric about Prida was extremely stupid. Cuban-Americans who should have known better compared her to a Nazi, and justified their desire to banish her work from Miami by making the rather dubious claim that it was like letting a Nazi play appear in Miami Beach. Interestingly, this was not the first time Miami Cubans had used "Jewish" imagery to describe their situation. The Cuban-American "civil rights" organization FACE ("Facts About Cuban Exiles") was directly modeled on the Jewish Anti-Defamation League. Indeed, Cuban Miami's way of describing the Castro regime was as a "holocaust." But, equally, for Anglo Miamians to talk about censorship in a Cuban theatre sat a bit oddly on people most of whom had never set foot inside a Cuban theatre.

Still, however one looked at it, liberal Miamians could hardly be faulted for being appalled by the political transformation — a mad dash to the right, really — which the Cubans had effected in South Florida. It was a remarkable event. History, rather than progressing forward in its orderly, liberal way, was moving backward. Even in the bad old days of the Dixiecrat, straight-seg South, Dade County had been a liberal enclave. Since the days of Franklin Roosevelt, the area had been represented by one of the most liberal New Dealers of them all, Representative Claude Pepper. Certainly, once large numbers of liberal Jews from the North began to settle in South Florida after the Second World War, the region seemed closer politically to New York or New Jersey than to Palm Beach County a few miles to the north, let alone to the archreactionary central and northern parts of the state. In the nineteen-fifties, it was liberal Miami Beach Jews, like now State Senator Jack Gordon and his late wife, Barbara, who led the Civil Rights movement in Miami. Even as late as the nineteen-sixties, the political temper of Dade was overwhelmingly liberal. Inconceivable as it is in a time when the biggest thing in many middle-class Miami high schools is reserve officer training, Mitchell Kaplan remembers that as a student during the Vietnam War, his high school was full of New Leftists.

Had the Cubans not come to Miami, it is quite probable that the city would have become even more liberal under the twin prods of black unrest and urbanization. In time, one might have envisaged a political cross between New York and Atlanta with a better tax base. Instead, as Howard Kleinberg, the editor of the *Miami News*, told me, not entirely jokingly, "the last leftist in Dade County is hiding in a bomb shelter somewhere and liberals are getting pretty thin on the ground." The Miami Beach line that the county was a nice liberal place that got hijacked by a bunch of fanatical right-wing Cubans may be too simple, but it is easy to understand why people who remember the Klan in Dade County, the curfew for blacks on Miami Beach, and the cracker evangelists prattling on about "Fido Castro, Khrushchev's little puppy dog," should be horrified at having to refight every social battle of the last three decades all over again in Miami, this time with the clear prospect of losing.

Were this the gut of Anglo resentment, it would be easier to be sympathetic. But what Anglos resent about living in the new Miami dominated by Cuban-American politics and tastes transcends the daily tug of any particular issue, or the unsettling sight of a foreign flag flying over a pharmacy or the unsettling sound of an unfamiliar language at the supermarket checkout counter. Starkly put: if Anglo Miami is an interesting but not, perhaps, really a first-rate city, Cuban Miami, far from being just another sprawling ethnic enclave — a Chinatown under the palms — is a great capital city. All Cubans feel this and every Anglo knows they do. It is difficult to live in someone else's capital city, particularly if you were there first. The truth remains, however, that most Anglos are not simply Miamians but maintain deep sentimental ties to other cities in the United States. If they are Jews, many still cling to the memories of the New York from which they or their parents migrated. If they are white Southerners, many can still hark back to rural Georgia, Alabama, or to the Florida Panhandle way up in the northwestern part of the state. But the Cubans who left after Fidel Castro's revolution have only the memory of their island and, now, the lives they have made for themselves in Miami. These are the only places.

To be sure, the country of which Miami is the capital is an imaginary one, that of *el exilio*, of the Cuban diaspora. But, if anything, Miami's fictive quality only magnifies its place in the lives of most Cuban-Americans. Those who live elsewhere in the United States often talk about returning to Miami in much the same way American expatriates in Europe look forward to their trips home. Those who live in Europe find themselves coming back as well, however much they protest Miami's irrelevance to their new lives in Madrid, Barcelona, or Paris. To return to Miami is to reimmerse oneself in one's Cubanness. It is almost as if, anywhere else, that condition runs the risk of being diluted by forces in the outside world.

As for those who live in Miami, they seem to have a difficult time imagining life anywhere else. A Cuban teenager I met one night in Coconut Grove talked about his recent trip to Atlanta as if he were describing a canoe trip down the Amazon. Most of his friends had never seen snow except in movies or on rock videos. Many times after dinner, Cuban parents I met would look fondly across at their young children (usually, by then, happily engrossed in their video games) and say, brightly, "I'm sure they'll never want to leave Miami." In a community where people have old-fashioned family habits (children tend to live with their parents until they marry, nearby afterward), leaving is always seen as something of a desertion. And anyway, everything outside is *terra incognita*.

A university professor in the Midwest and one of the minority of Cubans to live outside the great Cuban-American centers of South Florida and New Jersey described Miami to an interviewer as the base of (Cuban) culture in the United States: "Miami is Mecca, and it is also Jerusalem." In his affecting novel *Our Life in the Last World*, the Cuban-American writer Oscar Hijuelos describes the life of the Santinios, an immigrant Cuban family in New York. Toward the end of the book, the hero, Hector, returns to Miami to visit his relatives. It is clear that, in returning to

Miami, Hector is reimmersing himself in his Cuban-ness even though in New York he lived among Cubans too. But they were poor people, leading the mean, difficult lives of the inner city. In Miami, Hector finds "no street gangs, derelicts, or junkies. No broken glass. He liked being near Cubans who did not stagger down halls; he felt protected. Strolling along the white sidewalks, under coconut and orange trees, he daydreamed about living this good life. . . . Here, in Miami, he stood at the edge of the water, thinking that Cuba was only 140 miles away."

Miami is the home of "fine Cubans." As for Hector, the people on the Calle Ocho barely recognize him as a Cuban at all. After all, if he does not live in Miami what proof is there of his authentic Cubanness? Walking along in Little Havana, Hector imagines what he will have to say to convince them:

> "Look, my mother believes in the spirits and the Devil and Jesus Christ. I know about Santa Barbara! And the Virgen del Cobre! I know about the white cassava and yucca and arroz con pollo y lechón asado . . . Machado and Máximo Gómez . . . and my father came from San Pedro, Oriente Province, home province of Fidel Castro, Batista, and Desi Arnaz. My father's a worker and Santiago is fifty miles south of Holguín. I know about the shadows and magic, how you court nice girls and get married, and drink only with the men, and the women are your slaves, and you look to the future and never fear death. You have the Day of the Three Kings instead of Christmas as the time for giving presents . . ." and on and on, until he felt himself fading away.

Of course, what Hector really has to do is not recite all these ethnographic tidbits but move back to Miami, the only place outside Cuba itself Cubans have a right to call home.

Even Cuban-Americans who detest Miami, who call it "the ghetto," rail at its reactionary conformism, and sedulously refuse to return, seem every bit as obsessed with the place as people who have never gone farther north than the Broward County line. When they tell you in New York or Toronto how much they hate the place, these Cubans are reminiscent of no group as much as of those American Jews who constantly go around telling people how un-Jewish they feel. "As you walk down Eighth Street," a Cuban professional man in his early forties who lives in New York told José Llanes, "in a sense you have entered a time capsule that has transported you to the past. In Miami, Cubans live or try to live *la Cuba de ayer*, the Cuba of yesterday. It is a mythical country we have fabricated, where nostalgia and myth abound."

The only myth that abounds in Anglo Miami is the myth of the fine weather. On my return to Miami, I stared through the cab window into the rain-swept street. As myths went, there was no contest. On LeJeune Boulevard, we passed the familiar toy-castle-shaped exterior of a restaurant called El Cid. Under the granite stanchions of Metrorail, a *marielito* with a glazed look stood languidly offering to sell single sprigs of jasmine. He had the cuffs of his jeans rolled up in a style that had been popular in the United States in 1959; that was the year fashion stopped in Cuba. After a bit, the cab looped back toward Southwest Miami. What better way to punctuate my first day back in Miami than with a cup of coffee at the Versailles, preferably in the back room called the Hall of Mirrors.

THERE IS A MAN in Little Havana, a slight, intense, elderly fellow with a decided proclivity for shiny polyester suiting and wide, resolutely unfashionable ties, who never leaves his house even to go to the local market without bringing with him, cradled in his arms, his most cherished possession: a faded portrait of General Fulgencio Batista y Zaldívar, the man Fidel Castro drove out of the Presidential Palace in Havana on January 1, 1959. Curiously, though Batista owned a house in Daytona Beach, Florida, and had even lived in it during the late nineteen-thirties, after his first stint as Cuba's president, he never visited the United States after Castro overthrew him; Cubans in Miami like to tell you, wryly, that the general couldn't get a visa. Instead Batista died, rich even by the exigent standards of his fellow deposed tyrants, in 1973 at his villa in southern Spain.

In its first incarnation, at the beginning of the nineteen-sixties, Cuban Miami was overwhelmingly a *batistiano* city. This is hardly surprising. When the *barbudos*, Castro's army, entered Havana, Cubans had about had it with Batista. There was tremendous enthusiasm for the revolution. Castro kept insisting he was no communist and the Cuban middle class made the fatal error of believing him. And while they rather blindly went about their business, they had no idea that they would soon be following the late, unlamented members of the old regime's inner circle into exile in Florida. The first planeload of these was the one that had taken Batista and his immediate entourage toward the safety of the Trujillo family estate, otherwise known as the Dominican Republic. The second went north, carrying the persons, families, and loot of some of the most feared men in prerevolutionary Cuba to Jacksonville, Florida.

The most notorious among them was a torturer, Lieutenant Colonel Irenaldo García-Báez, the chief of SIM, Batista's secret police. Also on board was the Tabernilla family, whose nicknames came right out of a late-nineteen-forties Mexican cowboy picture. There was "Pancho," the head of the armed forces, "Winsy," the Air Force chief, and "Silito," Batista's military liaison officer. Only Dolores del Rio was missing from the flight manifest. But Rubén Batista, the general's eldest son, was a passenger, though he split off from the rest of the group the moment the plane landed on American soil. As it happened, none of these people proceeded immediately to Miami (although, of course, many later settled there), and the honor of being the first *batistiano* Miamian fell, a few days later, to one of Batista's senators, one José González Puente. In the months that followed, however, virtually all the important or infamous politicians and military officers who had served Batista (or at least those who had not been arrested by the revolutionary government) made their bedraggled way to South Florida. *Batistiano* Miami was born.

Today, that city lies submerged, buried like one of those Spanish galleons Florida treasure hunters are always searching for, under the many waves of Cuban immigration which were to follow. Still, the *batistiano* city is not difficult to locate even today. The faithful still celebrate September 4, the anniversary of that day in 1933 when then Army Sergeant Batista staged the first of his two successful coups d'état. And the frankly named Batistiano Armed Forces Social Club holds a regular Sunday meeting in a private dining room in a restaurant in Little Havana. But even their devotion to the general's memory and the *batistiano* cause pales before that of the man with the portrait.

He has grown old in that cause. The man with the portrait, who never, in fact, met Batista, although they corresponded, insists that, if anything, his belief in the general has grown deeper and stronger as the years have filed past. The man's name is José Manuel García, and, were it not for the portrait that he holds or carries fastened around his neck, he would be indistinguishable, seated at El Pub Calle Ocho or La Esquina de Tejas in Little Havana sipping his *café cortado*, from the other elderly gents who have stopped in for a quick cup at the counter. García earns his living as a Fuller Brush salesman, and the general accompanies him on his rounds through Southwest Miami. The portrait accompanies him everywhere.

Batista came from rural Oriente. Unlike Fidel Castro, whose father owned considerable land in that same region and who is as white as one gets to be anywhere south of Stockholm, Batista had black blood. As a young man, he was called *el mulatto lindo*, the handsome mulatto. It is one of the many paradoxes of Cuban history that the white, middle-class supporters in Oriente of Fidel Castro's 26th of July Movement

[155]

often carefully refrained from voicing their revolutionary opinions in front of their black and mulatto servants, who were, overwhelmingly, loyal to the general. Oriente Province is the home of Santería, the Afro-Cuban cult that was brought to the island by the first Yoruba slaves. The faith's book of rituals, the *Orisha*, is widely sold in Miami, where Santería flourishes, a seemingly incongruous element in the lives of otherwise business-oriented, impeccably upwardly mobile white Cubans. Only a block past Radio Station WQBA, "la Cubanisima," there sits a discreet little storefront *botánica*, a shop that sells the magic papers and potions of the cult. Most of the demand seems to be from women seeking to do something about their love lives. There is *Amansaguápos*, sworn to turn even the most brutish man tender, *Amárrame El Hombre*, which, it is said, will keep even the archest of Cuban philandering husbands faithful, and, since even Santería is not immune to the tribal styles of the American supermarket, an aerosol spray that contains seven potions in one.

The Anglos are certainly right about the ubiquity of Santería in Miami today. The cult is surging, and it is quite common to hear of people spending vast sums of money on offerings, services, and statuary. As one drives past the car dealerships, the gleaming bank buildings, and the bustling restaurants of Southwest Miami, one notices, pinned to telephone poles and to public benches, cheap leaflets announcing celebrations in honor of the Saints of *El Monte*, the mountain, home of the cult. These festivals are often held in halls or municipal centers which, on most days, host far more conventional gatherings. It is possible to attend a meeting of an anti-Castro group on

Monday, of a civic organization like the Rotary Club on Wednesday, and follow these more twentieth-century rituals with a celebration of *santerismo* at the weekend. (By now, the cleaning staff must be inured to absolutely every sensation.) Even many Cuban-Americans who profess no interest at all in Santería are protective about those who practice it, much the way rural Southerners unscathed by born-again Christianity reserve a sneaking admiration for those who have found Jesus in all these picturesque ways. They know it's tacky, in other words, but they don't feel entirely comfortable turning up their noses. Nor do I. "Santería," a pink-cheeked Cuban lawyer observed, cutting happily into his fairly convincing steak au poivre in one of the better French-like restaurants of North Miami Beach, "provides us Cubans with a spiritual dimension we lack in our business lives."

In a community that worships money more intently than Aaron did the Golden Calf, Santería, a hybrid religion that honors the earth and Africa (and is, of course, perfectly congruent with Christianity in the Caribbean) endures as the esoteric antinomy: Yoruba night to Catalán, consumerist day. To be a believer is to be able to enjoy that mystical communion with the animating spirits behind all living things which white people in Cuba believe to be the special realm of blacks. Even to come from Oriente Province, from that heavily black, desperately poor region of Cuba where the sugar cane is mostly harvested, is to partake, folkloristically at least, in the disciplines of these mountain saints. Or, at least, this is what the man with the portrait maintains about Batista. The general, he told a reporter from the *Miami Herald*, "came from Oriente, and so he was close to the earth."

According to García, Batista could work miracles by simply opening his mouth. In Cuba in the good old days, he insists, it would rain whenever Batista delivered a speech. "He had that gift," García says firmly. A few years ago, while Miami was suffering through a rare drought, García decided the general could help. "I said to myself," he recalled, "if Batista could only speak." Rigging a loudspeaker to the roof of his car, García drove slowly through the streets of Southwest Miami, spreading Batista's voice as if it were the fine spray of an aerosol potion from a local *botánica*. "Sure enough, it rained," García claimed staunchly, "and everyone said, 'Batista really did make it rain.'"

The man with the portrait is, of course, a glorious eccentric. There are even a few others of the same breed in Little Havana, though none is as interesting or as emblematic. The Bronze Penny, as he is called, hands out cigars which have a picture of Castro on the band; El Loco de la Calle Ocho (the nut from Eighth Street), as the local merchants so unceremoniously call him, has insisted for years that various American politicians are not in fact who they claim to be, but are rather Cubans from the Havana suburbs, planted in their high offices by Fidel Castro himself. Certainly the pleasure I felt in encountering these characters during my visits to Miami had nothing to do with believing they were representative. It was simply a relief to meet people whose large, impassioned exuberance could not, by the wildest stretch of the imagination, net them a dime. Moreover, the baroque impracticality of their beliefs, which in itself harked back to the great, showy looniness that flourished in Cuba before it got cold-soaked with communism, contrasted happily with the implacable, fanatic money-hungriness of Miami, particularly in its Cuban-American incarnation.

Sustained by his almost romantic devotion to Batista, the man with the portrait is able to practice the politics of exile as a serene, benign activity. Not only is there no violence to it, there is scarcely any collegiality. He takes a dim view of his fellow *batistianos*, in fact. When, every September 4, the faithful gather, García is notable by his absence. "I don't just honor Batista once a year," he explained indignantly to a reporter. "I am the man who carries Batista in my hand every day. For me, every day is the Fourth of September."

It would be lovely, of course, if the man with the portrait were simply a charming fantasist whose views found no graver echo in the larger community. Alas, in Miami the serious politics of exile attract many fantasists, none of whom, understating the matter dramatically, could remotely be thought of as benign. Arguably, the American-born generations who are now reaching adulthood may be less concerned with *La Causa*, the determination to topple Castro and return to the island. But even for those in their thirties and forties who grew up in the United States, the dream dies hard. It is not as if, as in the case of the White Russian émigrés in Paris, that age will eventually put paid to the movement. To be sure, particular factions among the exiles will disappear (*batistiano* Miami is already moribund, as is, largely, the Miami that harkens back to the presidency of the liberal Ramón Grau San Martín), but with Cuba so near and the refugees still streaming north to Miami, there is no real reason to suppose that the drama of the Cuban diaspora will ever completely disappear. Indeed, were it not for the fact that Castro and, for that matter, his regime are mortal, it would be possible to envisage, generations on, that Cuban-Americans would still be repeating, "Next year in Havana" in the manner of pious Jews. Leaving such fancies aside, Cuban Miami today is indecipherable without seeing the centrality of these terrible passions of exile.

If, for the *batistiano* old guard, every day is the Fourth of September, the overwhelming majority of Miami Cubans are fixed on another date or, more precisely, on three days, April 17, 18, and 19, 1961. On the seventeenth, Brigade 2506, a CIA-backed force of 1,400 Cuban exiles, landed on the beaches of the Bay of Pigs in Southwestern Cuba. By April twentieth, they had met with crushing defeat at the hands of the Cuban army and people. The invasion force, a mix of ex-*batistiano* soldiers and other, more simply anti-Castro refugees (the political directorate of the invasion force was led by figures like ex-President Miró Cardona, an anti-Castro politician), had expected that there would be a mass uprising amongst the Cuban people. The Americans had assured them that adequate air and naval support would be provided.

The Cuban people disappointed the *brigadistas*; not only didn't they rise up, they fiercely supported the Castro government. As for the Americans, it did not take the soldiers on the beach very long to realize that they had been betrayed by their American mentors. The 1,200 survivors of Brigade 2506 were paraded gleefully on Cuban television, but, with a few exceptions, there were no atrocities. A few of the leaders were imprisoned in Cuba, but rather than sentence the invaders to long prison terms, the Castro government held them for ransom. A year and a half later, they were exchanged for fifty-three million dollars' worth of food and medicine. It had been a complete fiasco from every point of view.

On December 29, 1962, the veterans of the invasion force, who had been returned to Miami the week before, mustered in the Orange Bowl stadium. Before a crowd of forty thousand weeping, shouting, defiant supporters, they presented the flag of the brigade to President Kennedy. Some people are slow learners. "I can assure you," Kennedy shouted, "that this flag will be returned to this brigade in a free Havana." The air rang with fervor, Spanish, and, over the loudspeaker, the nasal *a* of Boston. The crowd began to shout, "*Guerra*," war; the crowd began to shout, "*libertad*," freedom. Jacqueline Kennedy came up to the rostrum and, in her fluent Castilian Spanish, assured the *brigadistas* that she would instruct her small son John about their courage. In 1976, brigade veterans had to hire lawyers to get the flag back from the U.S. government. It had been stored in a crate in the basement of the Kennedy Library in Waltham, Massachusetts.

Cuban Miami has not yet recovered from the lies it was told at the time of the Bay of Pigs. To some extent, it has taken refuge in lying to itself. "We were betrayed," the line goes; "had it not been for the American failure of will we would be back in Havana." Conveniently forgotten in all this is the fact that the Cuban people not only didn't rise up at the time of the Bay of Pigs, they showed no particular interest in aiding the various guerrilla movements that arose in the nineteen-sixties. The credo in Miami is that there are only two forces in Cuban life, Castro

[161]

and the exiles. Curiously, the only other place this view is asserted is Havana itself. As the exiles cleave to their "vertical" line of intransigent refusal to have anything to do with Castro, the maximum leader brandishes a mythicized version of *batistiano* Miami to keep his own reformers at bay.

Miami, of course, is nothing like the blood-soaked fantasies put out over Radio Havana. Today, the city is as full of people who opposed Batista's rule as of those who served it. Some of the leaders of Castro's Second Front of the Escambray mountains live in Dade County. One of their leaders, Max Lesnik, runs a glossy magazine called *Réplica*, which blends celebrity profiles with surprisingly liberal politics. The nonrevolutionary opposition to Batista, including members of the *Ortodoxo* party, which was briefly allied with Castro, is present as well. Carlos Prío, the president of Cuba whom Batista overthrew in 1952, lived in Miami until his suicide in 1977; Tony Varona, another former prime minister (he tried, when Castro's victory was imminent, to form a "third force"), lives in retirement in Hialeah.

Indeed, it is impossible to drive through Southwest Miami without wondering, as one passes the neat bungalows and Spanish-style ranch houses, whether the middle-aged Cuban out watering his car is in fact a former member of Batista's security forces or a veteran of the *Directorio*, the urban resistance to the Batista regime. Sometimes, at the bar of a restaurant, I would see a man in smoked glasses I would have bet my last cent was a torturer, but, mostly, in the Miami of today, it is impossible to tell who did what. After twenty-seven years, it is not entirely clear that even the principals themselves remember accurately what they did, which side they were on. Exile is the place where everyone rewrites the past. Sometimes, in the Versailles or across the street at La Carreta, two men who have obviously not liked each other for a very long time will meet. But in these relatively pacific nineteen-eighties, nothing more untoward takes place in these encounters than an *abrazo* — that somewhat absent-minded embrace to which Latin men are given, a greeting in which the two celebrants pat each other soundly on the back while looking off into some middle distance, as if distracted by an errant thought. It looks like nothing so much as a rather perfunctory weapons check. In Miami, even today, it probably often is.

When the British travel writer Jan Morris went to Miami, her Dominican chauffeur warned her about Cubans. "Them Cubans can certainly talk," he said. "Yappety-yappety-yap — that's what Cubans is all about." Talk doesn't mean much in the British West Indies; in Little Havana, it matters what people say about you. More particularly, it matters if they say, hint even, that you're a communist. Every restaurant in Cuban Miami seems to have piles of the so-called underground press, available for free in the entry hall. All the political permutations of the exile world are on display in the pages of these little scandal sheets, whose names run from the marmoreal *Girón* (the organ of Brigade 2506) to the fiery *Patria* to the rather pining *El Ausente*, the absent one. And it is not, as they are wont to say in Little Havana, good for business to get called a communist in one of these papers; there is no smear that sticks longer. (Several people claimed that it was through this kind of extortionate prodding that the papers got their ads. In effect, the proposition was "Take out an ad or I'll start saying you were a communist back in the old days." It's cheaper to give in.)

The world of the underground press, though wholly unlike that of *Miami Mensual* and the Cuban Chamber of Commerce, was still not entirely separable from it. The two discourses were like adjacent Havana neighborhoods, or a mansion and its servants' quarters. The fact remains that all political discussion in Cuban Miami is, at least publicly, moored securely on the extreme right. In part, this is the result of a minority of vocal extremists constantly accusing everyone else of being soft on Castro, with the result that with a few notable exceptions people spend a good deal of time reasserting their own intransigence, their "verticality." At the same time, however, the political cohesion of Cuban Miami resided quite simply in the shared sense of community brought on not only by exile but by the impression of continuity between life in Cuba and life in Dade County. The Cubans might be in exile, but they also felt they had taken the island with them when they left. Of the one hundred twenty-six townships that existed in pre-Castro Cuba, one hundred fourteen have their own civic associations in Miami. One sees the signs of the very real refusal to take geographical reality into account all over the place. At the edge of Coral Gables, I noticed a sign advertising "The Caballero Funeral Home, Founded 1858." Miami, of course, did not exist in 1858, and I realized with a start that the owners meant founded *in Havana* in 1858. It is as if Cuban Miami recapitulates all the particles of prerevolutionary Havana, with, of course, the hated exception of the left. The left stayed home and ate the country.

To be sure, there are hints of change. Young Cuban-Americans often insist privately that when the older generation dies attitudes will shift dramatically. The problem is that, almost invariably, they immediately tell you something that makes you think they're wrong, for example that they have a brother in 2506 or that they are just back from school in Philadelphia. Cuban moderates are right to be cautious. Being a liberal in Miami is somewhere between being a member of a secret society and being a member of an endangered species. And though the West Indian who took Jan Morris around might sneer about Cuban "yapping," the threat is by no means entirely verbal. In the early nineteen-seventies, a group of young Cuban-American leftists formed an organization called the Antonio Maceo Brigades. They traveled to Cuba, where they were feted; then they returned to Miami, where they were not. Within months, one of the leaders of the group had been killed and the organization was in a shambles. There were other casualties. In 1974, a young Cuban named Luciano Nieves used the pages of Lesnik's *Réplica* (which itself has been bombed several times) to call for a rapprochement between the exiles and Castro. Nieves was murdered in the parking lot of Variety Children's Hospital in Miami in 1975.

From a practical point of view, liberal Cubans can choose either to eschew politics altogether while waiting for the actuarial tables to work their magic (many have opted for this), or to get out of town. Either way, for people with such views Miami is a fearsome place indeed. Marifel Perez-Estable, one of the editors of *Areito*, a left-leaning Spanish-language magazine in New York, told an interviewer for the *Miami Herald* that it was hard for people like herself to live in Miami. "Everybody knows everything," she said, "and it makes it difficult for those who are 'fingered' as having a pro-Castro position to do something as simple as going to the market." Was that a Cuban-American euphemism for continuing to breathe?

Even as rich and as influential a figure as the banker Bernardo Benes has found himself at risk. Benes is a "Jewban," a member of the Jewish community of Havana, which, for all intents and purposes, exists only in Florida. It was Benes who, during the nineteen-seventies, propounded the idea of a dialogue with the Castro regime. Worse, he returned to Cuba. According to the doctrine of Little Havana, a Cuban is not supposed to return to talk, he is supposed to return as a liberator. Benes, in his practical way, used his contacts in Havana to good effect during the Mariel boatlift. It is only recently that he has stopped wearing a bulletproof vest. As far as most people I met in Southwest Miami are concerned, the man is an agent of Fidel Castro.

Even the unwary visitor can run into trouble because of the wrong associations in Miami. At a party in Key Biscayne, I was introduced as the editor of a number of Latin-American writers.

"Like who?" my host inquired, a rather indecipherable expression creasing his features.

Trying to play it safe, I groped for a writer who would be politically acceptable. "Mario Vargas Llosa," I replied, hoping Mario would forgive me.

"He's a communist," my host exclaimed.

At this point, the friend who had brought me to the party intervened. "No, no, Jorge," he said, "you're thinking of Carlos Fuentes."

"Him too," said my host with equal inaccuracy, and then, with a great laugh, clapped me on the shoulder and handed me a topping glass of rum and Coke, that drink they call a Cuba libre.

Had I been a Cuban-American, I am by no means sure that things would have turned out so happily. Perhaps I'm wrong. It was a beautiful night, cloudless and starry, and the band on the verandah was hot. My host went out to dance with his daughter, starting to do the samba even as he moved away from the bar toward the open french doors that gave on to the bay. He waved to me, irony and genuine, hospitable warmth chasing each other across his broad features, as he sashayed deftly into the dancing throng.

In his invaluable *Diary of the Cuban Revolution*, Carlos Franquí, who ran the revolutionary radio station in the Sierra Maestra, and was one of Fidel Castro's closet collaborators before he too went into exile, wrote of Cubans:

> A good Cuban is one who possesses the rhythm of the black, who dances well, and is as delirious as a Spaniard but a bit more graceful; one who thinks like a Frenchman, believes in gambling luck as the Chinese, is as much of a Don Juan as if he were an Italian, does not like the gringos, is a chatterbox, and is also capable of embarking on *anything*.

Under a full Miami moon, a mile from where Richard Nixon used to live, I watched the Cubans dance and dance.

IF ANYBODY over eighteen is doing much dancing in the black neighborhoods of Northwest Miami, in the black section of Coconut Grove, or in the virtually all-black town of Opa-Locka a few miles north of the city, it is more likely to be because they are out of work or determinedly high than because they find being black in Miami anything to dance about. Cubans might choose to claim, with Carlos Franquí, to have the rhythm of blacks, but in Miami they tended to have the incomes of whites, which has rather a large, salutary effect on the old natural exuberance. In an America so absorbed with the pleasures of money and a metastasizing letch for material things that when a New York magazine called *M* — "the magazine for the civilized man" — devoted a cover story to greed, most people I knew assumed the editorial position would be favorable, blacks are of necessity out of fashion. And blacks are Miami's dirty little secret, though their presence there is as old as the city itself.

When Miami was incorporated in 1896, one hundred sixty-two of the three hundred sixty-eight voting residents were black. Indeed, the first blacks to settle in Dade County had come there from South Carolina in the early part of the century; the second large black migration had come from the Bahamas soon after. Most of them went to Coconut Grove, which even today, as development has transformed the Grove into one vast condominium, a Fortress Yuppie on the shores of Biscayne Bay, retains a substantial black population. But it was the construction of Henry Flagler's railroad, and, in its wake, the first tourist boom, that lured large numbers of black people to South Florida from the plantations and tenant farms of Georgia. The new arrivals settled, for the most part, in Overtown, then called Colored Town, a segregated section somewhat north of downtown Miami carved out for the purpose from the vast lands deeded to the city of Miami by the two great landholders of nineteenth-century Dade County, Julia Tuttle and Mary Brickell. In 1898, the U.S. Army began to use a nearby military base, Camp Miami, as a staging area for its operations in Cuba and Puerto Rico against the forces of the King of Spain. The white soldiers were given to crossing into Colored Town, where they beat up the locals with impunity. At least one black, and probably more, was killed by them.

By the beginning of the century, blacks were well over forty percent of Miami's population. The *Miami Herald* and its now defunct competitor, the *Miami Metropolis*, were no better than the times and railed about the "coons" and the "hamfats." But black Miami kept growing. By the nineteen-twenties, the era of the great Florida landboom and, coincidentally, of the revival of the Ku Klux Klan, conditions in Colored Town, which had never been very good, grew dire. Disease and crime were rampant. (Colored Town wasn't only referred to as "Darktown," it was literally dark at night, for, unlike white Miami, the area was not yet electrified.) This was the same period during which Addison Mizner was building his Salamancan palaces a few miles away in Coral Gables and when Glenn Curtiss, one of the early pioneers of aviation in the United States, was constructing the new city of Opa-Locka, where each section would reflect, in its street names and its architecture, a different tale from the Arabian Nights. Carl Fisher's hotels were bursting with Northern holidaymakers, though, of course, there was a dawn-to-dusk interdict against blacks setting foot in Miami Beach. Blacks were loathed in Miami, but, however much the city fathers tried to discourage the burgeoning black population, Colored Town was becoming simply too small, and conditions in the area too degraded, for things to go on indefinitely as they were.

It was not out of simple patriotism alone that so many black parents in the nineteen-thirties named their children after Franklin Delano Roosevelt. In 1934, in the wake of a series of articles in the by now more liberal *Miami Herald*, national attention was brought to bear on the plight of the black residents of Miami's Colored Town. Roosevelt ordered the federal Works Project Administration to investigate conditions in there. The result, three years later, was the construction of the first federally funded public housing project in the southeastern United States. It was built along 12th Avenue between Northwest 62nd and 67th streets, separated, at first, by a wall from the white neighborhood adjoining it. The project was called Liberty Square.

By the nineteen-fifties, Liberty City had grown into a large black neighborhood. The whites who had lived near the original Liberty Square had long ago moved away and the district had become the "middle-class" black neighborhood, even as Overtown remained both the slum and something of a cultural mecca, particularly for live jazz. Both areas were, of course, still segregated. It was an era of change, even in Jim Crow Miami (though things moved rather slower than people in Dade County like to pretend they did today). The public schools were integrated in 1959. In 1961, the first black students were admitted to the University of Miami. But just as black people were slowly and painfully achieving some measure of enfranchisement in the City of Miami, the Cuban refugees began to arrive in large numbers.

There was no possibility that a largely uneducated black population would be able to compete successfully with these well-educated, middle-class immigrants, despite the fact that the new arrivals were mostly penniless and spoke no English. Within a year Cubans had begun taking over many of the jobs blacks had traditionally occupied. Instead of black waiters in the hotels of Miami Beach, there were Cubans; and in small retail businesses, the Cubans, a nation of shopkeepers if ever there was one, moved into and virtually took over a sector blacks were only beginning to enter. Only the jobs of porters at Miami International Airport and longshoremen in the port of Miami remained firmly in black hands. As early as 1966, Martin Luther King came to Miami and recognized the hostility that had arisen between the two groups over jobs. He was right, of course. As one Anglo Miamian recalled it, "Why should racist whites continue to hire blacks when there were all those white Cuban hands available to do the menial work?"

Within a decade, the traditionally black service jobs in Miami and Miami Beach had become almost entirely Hispanic. In such situations, there is rarely any going back. People don't get hired out of some general labor pool but through personal contacts with someone who can put in a good word with the employer. In other words they are hired because A recommends B; and in Miami José does not tend to recommend Kareem. A decade later, the Cubans had soared away from these menial jobs, but, instead of the sector becoming black once again, it was other Hispanic immigrants from Central America or the Caribbean who replaced them. These immigrants, often illegal aliens, came cheaper than American blacks (this is why, for example, the only blacks one sees in these hotels are Haitians). Moreover, it was by now often Cuban managers who were doing the hiring, and they were more comfortable hiring, if not their fellow Cubans, then at least their linguistic compatriots. The blacks were frozen out, excluded by Cuban clannishness, the undercutting effect of illegal migration, and the Spanish language. When, in the mid-nineteen-seventies, Vernon Jordan addressed the annual meeting of the Urban League in Miami Beach, he observed angrily that the next time the organization returned to Miami, *if* it returned, he hoped he would see some black hands among those doing the serving.

One of the remarkable things about visiting Miami is that one rarely sees blacks in the jobs they hold in most American cities. But the pattern that is so crudely visible in Miami of newer immigrants having superseded blacks is in fact a fairly general one throughout the country. In New York and Washington, for example, black resentment against Korean and Chinese grocers is on the rise. The effect of all this is, in some sense, the dilution of the claims of black people on the United States. After all, when the civil rights movement began, black leaders like Martin Luther King could think of the United States in fairly simple terms. The country was ninety percent white and ten percent black. King's genius was to realize that his success depended on mobilizing the sluggish conscience of at least a good part of the white majority. Were he beginning today, the calculus would be far more complicated. King was lucky, in a sense, that the dawning of the civil rights struggle coincided with a period when there was relatively little immigration to the United States. One paroxysm of assimilation had ended; another, the one we are living through now, had not yet begun. Americans felt "American," and, however reluctantly, responsible for what had happened to black people. It is surely no accident that while the nation was being racked by civil rights demonstrations it was celebrating on a massive scale the hundredth anniversary of the Civil War.

One of the unexpected results of the arrival of so many Hispanic immigrants has been to make the black claim seem somehow fuzzier. Mention the Middle Passage, and liberals often seem to want to talk about the Mexican-American War. One can't keep every injustice in one's head at once; the claims contend with each other for the nation's attention. Moreover, as colored immigrants, particularly the Asians, do well in the United States, resentment starts to set in. If the West Indians can make it, what's wrong with the blacks? runs the argument. In this version, the new round of mass immigration serves as a lopsided vindication of the deep-rooted antiblack feeling, which never went away in the first place.

Miami is special because the Cubans were, in a way, the outriders for the great Third World immigration. Until the Cubans were allowed in, no people from the so-called Third World had been admitted to the United States legally in large numbers since the Mexicans in the nineteen-thirties. And most of them, infamously, had been deported. As for the Cubans themselves, they saw no particular reason to have to assume the burden of America's historical obligation to black people and remained largely indifferent to the situation in Northwest Miami. In any event, the Cubans reasoned, they were going back to Havana. More often than not, rich Cuban women were slightly puzzled by the fact that their maids couldn't ride next to them on the public buses. They felt rather liberal by contrast to Anglo Miamians.

Even today, most surveys suggest that Miami Cubans do not believe that there is racism in employment or housing. Those Cubans who do seem genuinely concerned with the situation of black people tend to think of themselves as Hispanic, not Cuban; and such people are easier to find in New York than they are in Miami. In South Florida, one almost has the feeling that the Cubans wonder what these black people are doing in this second Havana. That, of course, is the key. Cubans, who are no more racist than any other group of whites in North America, in fact have an intimate connection with black culture. But it is black Cuban culture, particularly in music, the preeminent Cuban art form both in Havana and in Miami, that affects them. The Cuban response to the black *mar-ielitos* was intense; the Cuban response to black Americans has been largely to pretend they don't exist. To do otherwise would be to abandon that special idea of Miami as a second Cuba.

As for the other recent Hispanic, Haitian, and Asian immigrants, they are indifferent as well. These people, after all, don't so much live in America as work in Miami. It is all very well for a few radical black intellectuals to natter on about the solidarity of all Third World peoples in the New World. The reality is that the immigrants have come to make good, not to make politics. And the dirty truth is that they often have no reason to love the black people they run into, since in Miami, as in the other central cities of America, blacks and the new immigrants live in separate neighborhoods, so that the principal contact is often between immigrant shopkeepers and the feral youth of the black underclass. Nor are blacks particularly fond of the newcomers. In Miami high schools black teenagers call each other "Haitian" when they want to be wounding, while late at night in Southwest Miami otherwise sunny Honduran cabdrivers mutter grimly in Spanish about refusing to pick up *los negros.*

Black Miami is like a tragic volcano. In the ninety-odd years the city has existed, this volcano has erupted in rage, pain, and murderous, invariably self-mutilating spasms of violence. All to no avail. After things quiet down, people put their newly acquired pistols and shotguns away and go on with their lives as if there were nothing to be learned, nothing to be understood or considered in the wake of what had happened. In the final reckoning, most Miamians don't believe there is anything more to be done about the blacks than there is about the hurricanes that from time to time lash the city. But hurricanes dissolve; Liberty City festers.

Blacks rioted in Miami for the first time in August 1968, during the same week that the Republican Party was nominating Richard Nixon for President over in Convention Hall in Miami Beach. Even as the candidate was promising the cheering delegates that "the dark long night for America [was] about to end," the streets of Miami were, literally, on fire. Reporters who covered the convention recall walking over to North Bay Road, on the western edge of Miami Beach, and looking across Biscayne Bay to where the palls of smoke were rising over downtown Miami. A police lieutenant said at the time that the firefights were as intense as in Vietnam. Six blacks were killed; half the shops in Overtown were looted.

In June of 1970, there was the so-called rotten-meat riot, the outgrowth of a protest against a white-owned store in Brownsville, a subdivision adjacent to Liberty City, which, local residents claimed, sold spoiled food. Two blacks dead in that one. And throughout the nineteen-seventies, there ensued a series of riots, near riots, and, most worryingly to white Miami, seemingly spontaneous eruptions of random stone-throwing at whites passing in their cars through the streets of the ghetto. Black Miami trembled in its rage, but it did not explode (though it was only a matter of time) until, in May of 1980, in the wake of the acquittal of the white policemen accused of murdering a black salesman called Arthur McDuffie, it blew up like a fireball.

This was the first time that the violence engulfed white lives as well as white property. Gangs of rabid teenagers, egged on by approving adults on the street corners, stalked the boulevards, stopping the cars driven by whites, dragging the people out, beating and sometimes killing them. Black Miami straddles many of the major roads which lead out of the city, and middle-class commuters heading to or from the northern suburbs regularly pass through. Time, the bitter old joke runs, is so that everything can happen; space is so that it all doesn't happen to you. On May 17 an innocent choice of route proved fatal for a number of innocent whites. Some were killed, many more horribly injured. Certainly, the black thugs drew no distinction between Anglo and Cuban whites. Indeed, in their excellent book *The Miami Riot of 1980*, Bruce Porter of Brooklyn College and Marvin Dunn of Florida International University observe matter-of-factly that "seven [of the victims] were white; an eighth victim, a light-skinned immigrant from Guyana . . . may well have been mistaken for a Cuban."

Indeed, the riot was without question as anti-Cuban as it was anti-Anglo. Cubans had not only replaced blacks in the jobs they had formerly occupied, they were seen as having unfairly been allowed to take over small businesses in Miami as well. In 1960, for example, blacks owned twenty-five percent of the gas stations in Dade County; in 1979, the year before the riot, the figure was nine percent. In the same period, the percentage of Cuban-owned filling stations had risen from twelve percent to forty-eight percent. Cuban entrepreneurial skill was not the sole explanation, whatever the Cubans believed. The Small Business Administration had a lot to do with it. From 1968 to 1979, Hispanics received forty-seven percent of the total of small business loans while black Miamians got only a little over six percent. As Dunn and Porter remark pointedly, this translates as "blacks, whose strength in the population is half that of Hispanics, [receiving] only one-seventh of what the Hispanics got from the SBA."

In 1982, there was another riot. This time the policeman doing the shooting was a Cuban. Miamians, as if cauterized by the 1980 riot, didn't even react all that strongly. They bought more guns, installed more burglar alarm systems and window grills (at night Miami houses are barred and gated like the prisons in the drawings of Piranesi), talked apocalyptically among themselves and on the radio call shows in both English and Spanish. They fretted that tourism would be affected, but, as far as the causes of the rioting were concerned, they more or less stopped worrying once the fires had been extinguished, the glass swept from the streets by crews of burly Hispanics on the municipal payroll, and the roads once again safe to traverse. When Miami returns to normal, the blacks disappear. They scarcely signify even in the Anglo nightmares about the Third World, those fears so brilliantly evoked by the film *Blade Runner*, which shows a Los Angeles of the not too distant future peopled almost entirely by a mix of Mexicans and Asians speaking a patois of Spanish, Japanese, and English. There are no blacks in that film (where did Watts go?), as there are none to speak of in the local versions of *Blade Runner* Anglo Miami was concocting in its imagination. Invisible man indeed.

Along Grand Avenue in Coconut Grove, numbed black children in running shoes and orange safety jackets weave amid the commuters' cars, hawking copies of the *Miami News*. On Biscayne Boulevard in Liberty City, black hookers wearing heels so high they wobble when they mean to wiggle leave their curbside perches to approach single white men in passing cars. In these AIDS-haunted days, even their come-ons seem to ooze self-hatred. "I've got a bargain for you today," they'll often say, without the slightest trace of irony, gesturing at the cheap motels that squat garishly on either side of the roadway. The bargain, usually declined ("We're not getting the business we should," one of these women said to me), is of course their own flesh. Off the main drags, one sees not only the project housing and the run-down apartment blocks graffitied to death, but shanties that seem to defy history and date back to slavery times. Middle-aged women, their arms pendulous and thick, puff asthmatically on their porches.

A gang of kids, the oldest no more than fourteen, shoots by on skateboards cursing. Their leader screams, "You can't stop me, I'm coming through" at no one in particular. The street is empty. The car that had been parked at the intersection now begins to move slowly up the street; a Playboy pendant swings from the rearview mirror. The two male occupants in the front seat seem to be looking for someone. From doorways, windows, and from radios the size of night tables perched on the hoods of rusty old Dodges, the rap music, the chant of a mugger or a lunatic, blasts away. Poor neighborhoods always seem hotter than rich ones. As I sit in my taxi, I wonder if it can really be the same temperature over in Key Biscayne. The driver wants to go back. As he turns down Seventh Avenue, I see a group of teenagers breakdancing until the effect in the haze has the same quality as slow motion; then the dance turns into a brawl. An old woman, her face all brown folds and puzzled indignation, moves slowly past them on her walker. She keeps her eye firmly on the empty, rubble-strewn lot on the opposite side of the street.

Overtown is half deserted now. It used to call itself the Harlem of the South when the claim meant something to be proud of. When the white movie theatres along Flagler Street could claim no distinction greater than that *Carnival in Costa Rica* had premiered at one, *Slattery's Hurricane* at a second, and *Storm over the Everglades* at a third, Overtown could boast the best jazz clubs south of Memphis. One day in Miami, an old-time resident of the district took me for a drive through its bulldozed streets. Pointing at an empty lot, he told me, "All the greats used to come here to play. Ellington. Basie. You name 'em, they were here." Then the man gave a sniffle and I quickly looked away, down another semi-burned-out side street. "Now it's just a garbage pit," he said, his anger having restored him. Later I asked him where his family lived. "Mobile," he replied, and, seeing my startled expression, or, perhaps just carried away by his own tale, insisted, "That's right, Mobile, Alabama. Bet you never thought you'd hear a man of color say that. But Mobile's paradise for a black man compared with Miami." And he went on to tell me how the Cubans had taken over his city.

Not being a black man, I could return to paradise without having to leave town. On the way back to the hotel, the radio was blaring on about how, in Opa-Locka, members of a sect called the Black Hebrews, who claimed to be the true Israelites and whose leaders had only recently been deported back to the U.S. from their commune in the Negev Desert, had killed two other blacks in a dispute in a housing project. The police, the reporter said, were helpless. The Black Hebrews were taking over in Opa-Locka. They were ruthless, and, besides, their business — a food store called the Jahweh Market — was one of the few thriving concerns in the neighborhood. While my cab was still in Liberty City, the news made sense, conformed to what I could see around me. But as we crossed the causeway heading toward Key Biscayne it became harder and harder to believe the story on the radio. The news commentator was recalling that, earlier in the year, a Liberty City shopkeeper named Prentice Rasheed, who had been burglarized eight times in the preceding year, had installed an electrified mesh under the roof of his store. A burglar had broken in and been electrocuted. "We live in a war zone here in Miami," Rasheed's lawyer had said, and the grand jury refused to pass an indictment. A Hispanic bellhop rushed to open the door for me at the entrance to the Sonesta Beach Hotel. It was twenty degrees cooler.

Down by the pool, as a bunch of pink, peeling baby arbitragers sipped their piña coladas and rehashed the Great American Real Estate Conversation, I watched a pair of unbelievably sexy Venezuelan teenagers cavort gleefully near the diving board. A middle-aged man in street clothes — was he an uncle, a bodyguard? — watched them keenly, sipping a single espresso and smoking. With their breasts practically popping out of their black string bikinis, and their arms stacked up to the elbows in Cartier, they were visions straight out of "Miami Vice." Even the arbitrageurs noticed eventually, although, as if on some kind of alternating current, they could neither quite tear themselves away from their consideration of long-term versus short-term mortgages nor could they ignore Eros splashing away.

I didn't want to listen to the businessmen, and the girls seemed far too dangerous to approach, their minder having caught my eye and fixed me with a look that was far from friendly. As for black Miami, it was too horrible and sad to think about, or perhaps I was too cowardly to face up to the task. The best way to lose a thought is stare at a magazine. I went into the lobby, got a copy of *The New Yorker*, and brought it back to the pool. As I opened it, I remember thinking that if I just looked at the cartoons and the ads I would be reprieved from my agitation. Wrong as usual. Even advertisements can make you weep.

It was a special insert called "Island Heritage: Caribbean Vignettes," and it had been prepared especially for *The New Yorker*, or so the copywriters claimed, by a consortium of West Indian holiday interests ranging from the tourist boards of most of the islands to the principal air carriers and tour operators serving the area. The text of the brochure was adapted from one of the Fielding Guides to the Caribbean. It was a narrative so devoid of politics or history as to be starkly immoral, though not one American in a thousand would have deemed it so except under very peculiar conditions like the ones in which I encountered it. Yet on the second page, there was a picture of a fat black woman with a basket of bananas on her head and a guitar in her hands.

Of course, who could fault the islands for trying to get more tourists? It was that or starve. And yet one strangled on the lies as one read. The anguished history of the Dominican Republic was summarized as "complex and convoluted, the Dominican Republic had a clear claim to Columbus." Though a few lines were devoted to the institution of slavery in the West Indies, this took the form (the example comes from the entry on Martinique) of such gnomic utterances as "after the freeing of the slaves in . . ." or, at most, of some cursory acknowledgment of the fact of slavery, usually subsumed in a paragraph about how the various "cultural influences" of slaves, Indians, and planters had created an exciting, or a cosmopolitan, or a relaxed atmosphere, depending on which island was being described. No mention whatever of the Middle Passage. No mention of the great slaver admirals, Rodney and De Grasse, except as picturesque warriors from a bygone era, who, for some unaccountable and unimportant reason had been kind enough to leave behind them all those picturesque forts for the kids to get taken to while Mom and Dad went snorkeling in the bay below, or, as the saying goes these days, enjoyed some "quality time" together.

(I suppose I was fortunate. *The New Yorker*, in its old-fashioned, enviably prudish way, still refuses to accept those kinds of advertisements from Caribbean island resorts whose come-on, basically, is "Why don't you two fabulous-looking people come down here right away and screw your brains out?")

But it was no good growing too indignant. It was a lot easier to feel sorry about the Caribbean than it was to attend to the cries of Overtown, something I seemed no more capable of doing on a consistent basis than the locals. It wasn't only bad faith. In Miami, the Caribbean insinuates itself into every thought. It shouts, "Here I am, right here, look," and before its thunderous, insistent tug black Miami receded; it was almost as if it belonged to the problems of another continent. Indeed, South Florida, as many writers had noticed, always seems in danger of drifting south into the Caribbean. In Liberty City, one forgets about the sea; it is an insignificant detail, no more germane to the situation of its residents than the Atlantic Ocean is for Harlem blacks. Once back on Key Biscayne, however, I could imagine little else. In almost any other port, the horizon is simply the more or less circular line that bounds the observer's view of the sea. In Miami, it was something quite different. The horizon there seemed like nothing so much as a peak or ridge, marked by a line of ships which, as if soldered to the spot, never seemed to progress toward their destination. But behind them, it was easy to imagine other ships waiting for night to fall so they could unload their cargoes of illegal men and drugs. Like a magnet, Miami drew the South up toward it.

That night, I went to a party in Coral Gables. Predictably, not even the servants were American blacks. People talked about their recent trips to London, about their children safely away in schools up North, about the frail health of their aged parents, and, inevitably, about the weather. Late in the evening, the hostess began to sing the praises of the Miami economy. "We're recession-proof down here," she said gleefully, "I mean down here things are just booming." Though her husband was looking on with a small frown, the woman plowed dauntlessly on. "I just love this great country of ours," she said to me. I wondered which one she was talking about.

A friend drove me back to Key Biscayne, and, when we got to the hotel, I invited her in for a nightcap at the bar, which, at the Sonesta Beach Hotel, is called Desires. The parking lot was solid with BMWs — "beamers" is what rich young Miamians call them — and the lobby turned out to be jammed with blond teenagers, spiffy and stoned in their pastel formal wear. It turned out the hotel was hosting a senior prom for one of the suburban high schools. Desires was inaccessible, so we walked down to the beach, picking our way past abandoned tartan cummerbunds, gold-flecked corsages, and the lovers who went with them. At the water's edge, someone had scrawled a message in the wet sand. I couldn't make it out and asked my friend what it said. "It's addressed to the Third World," she said sourly. "It says, 'Please don't take away our vacations.'"

IN THE BOARD GAME Monopoly, there is a space called Free Parking. At the opening of the game, before the players begin to gain control of the series of color-coded sets of property which make up most of the board, there is nothing particularly desirable about landing on this square. Indeed, the whole point is to get around the board quickly, hoping, with a few lucky rolls of the dice, to hit as many squares that are still for sale as possible. But, as the game progresses, and most of the properties are bought up, it becomes steadily more dangerous to throw the dice at all. Most of the squares are now laden with the "houses" and "hotels" built by one's opponents (the inventor of Monopoly, one Charles B. Darrow, had the New Jersey resort town of Atlantic City in mind when he invented the game in the nineteen-thirties; he could as well have been thinking of Miami Beach). To land on even one is to risk having to fork out such an exorbitant "rent" that it is quite possible to lose the game in a couple of turns. This is the moment, at the end of a game of Monopoly, when Free Parking comes into its own as the square on which everyone wants to land.

[186]

Miami is now the "Free Parking" of the rich of Latin America. For these people, in what may well turn out to be their "endgame," it is becoming steadily more perilous not only for them to land on someone else's property, but, in this age of ruinous inflation and pertinacious guerrillas, even for them to remain in the places they have always assumed were theirs. It was when large numbers of such people realized this that living in Miami came to appear all but irresistible. Whether it was the Bolivian tycoon living in his welter of bad art and gold-plated bathroom fittings in an estate on Key Biscayne, the Colombian jade dealer who had said good-bye to the dangers of Medellín (for sheer murderousness, the emerald business on the Colombian frontier makes that country's cocaine trade look positively tame by comparison) in favor of what must seem the positively trivial risks of Coconut Grove, or simply the wealthy businessman from Caracas who somehow managed to exchange his bolivares for dollars at a time when they were still worth something, and thus managed to hold on to his condominium on Brickell Avenue, all agreed that for a Latin American of means there was nothing like Dade County.

(Most of the illegal immigrants arrive in Miami with only what they can wear or what they can carry; social service workers will tell you that among the first things these new arrivals need to acquire are cheap clothes. Often, their choices ran to incongruously jolly T-shirts bearing the outlines of cartoon monsters or the logos of expensive sports cars and universities. When the prosperous Latin-Americans arrive at Miami International, they are, as their bankers and realtors hasten to inform you, preceded by the clatter of electronic money transfers and followed by their servants. Their children tend to go on to those same univer-

[187]

sities and drive those same hot cars that one saw advertised, whether with longing or indifference it was hard to tell, on the chests of Central American busboys in Coconut Grove or on the backs of Haitian cleaning ladies in Miami Beach.)

Miami has seen this process before, of course. Indeed, the transformation these rich Latin-Americans have effected is in many ways less startling, given the existence of Cuban Miami, than the migration during the nineteen-forties and -fifties of all those Northern Jews into a Miami Beach that had theretofore rigidly excluded them. Overnight, or so it must have seemed to people who were accustomed to the restricted hotels and "gentiles only" leasing clauses that had prevailed since Carl Fisher's day, Miami Beach became first a Jewish city and then a Jewish joke. Very much like the Cubans across the bay in Miami proper ten years later, the Jews did not so much adapt to their new surroundings as overrule, or even erase, them. Even today, Wolfie's Delicatessen on Collins Avenue in Miami Beach is all but indistinguishable from its counterparts in Manhattan or in Beverly Hills. "So I went down to Miami," a hundred Jewish stories begin. "So I went to see my folks, they live in Miami Beach now," are the opening words of countless Jewish family sagas. Even if the story is not a humorous one, the teller will likely as not get a laugh. For American Jews, there is something both vaguely embarrassing and vaguely comic even about the name of the place; it sounds odd, rather like those WASP names Sheldon, Myron, and Seymour, which American Jews adored fifty years ago because they seemed so quintessentially American and now sound so tinnily, quintessentially Jewish.

Today, Jewish Miami Beach squints uncomfortably across Biscayne Bay at Hispanic Miami. To be sure, the Jewish influence is still strong throughout Dade County. When José Saumat, a Cuban-American businessman from Hialeah, chose a name for his chain of appliance stores, he invented the fictional Anglo-Jewish partnership of "Kauffman & Roberts." North Miami Beach is still intensely Jewish, but though its residents include Isaac Bashevis Singer, the last great writer of the Yiddish language, the ambience of the place is Jewish only in that secular, Americanized way whose substance seems to consist of little more than a few shared tastes in food, a sprinkle of vivid Yiddish expletives, and a rather desperate, reflexive passion for the State of Israel. And South Miami Beach, once the last Jewish shtetl of Czarist Russia, is dying, if it has not died already. An ambitious commercial redevelopment plan undertaken (and then abandoned) in the late nineteen-sixties is partly to blame. It called for the razing of all but nine buildings south of Fifth Street and promised miracles. Inevitably, the result was further dilapidation. Indeed, the plan was so crassly imagined that, in a community full of Holocaust survivors, it spoke blithely of "relocation." After 1980, what community was left was all but destroyed by the newly arrived *marielitos*, the dregs of whom found their way to South Beach, where the elderly Jews were easy prey.

North Miami Beach is like a huge luxury shopping mall, but South Beach is being "gentrified." A few bright art historians and entrepreneurs declared that the retirement homes and cheap hotels along Ocean Drive were actually peerless examples of Art Deco architecture. The killer bees (i.e., the *marielitos*) having all but cleared the neighborhood, it was time for the (usually gay) worker bees to move in, opening boutiques and good restaurants. It is a nasty story, and a typical one. Old age may, as General de Gaulle once observed, be a shipwreck, but there is a particular horror to the scene along Ocean Drive or Collins Avenue in South Miami Beach. Ancient Jews walk painfully in the hot sun. Some are in a daze, others try to dress and walk jauntily, while still others stink of fear. From doorways, they are assailed by the incomprehensible epithets of young *marielito* thugs, while on the street corners they are practically blown back by the boom of jackhammers transforming their rest homes and synagogues into trendy hotels and discos. There are apartment complexes along Collins Avenue, whose owners, scenting the money that could come piling in if South Beach "works" (as in every neighborhood in gentrified urban America, the young lawyers and brokers eventually drive the gay worker bees out), have adopted the contemptible habit of offering a "yuppie" discount to renters under thirty-five.

But in fact it is the new arrivals from Latin America who are doing most of the renting. People say that it was Mexican Jews who bought up most of the supremely expensive condominiums in a self-contained development (it even has a moat) called Turnberry Isle off the northern tip of Miami Beach. In Miami proper, the bankrupt Venezuelans in the Arquitectónica buildings along Brickell Avenue seem to be selling out not to Anglos but rather to rich Central Americans. For other prosperous migrants, "Free Parking" is a condominium in Coconut Grove, perhaps the one which boasts units in the style of "London flats, Paris apartments, and New York lofts," or perhaps the Grove Island development in which the builder, Martin Margulies, camouflaged three fairly unprepossessing apartment blocks with tens of millions of dollars' worth of modern sculpture flung, either haphazardly or tastelessly, it is hard to tell, across the grounds. On Grove Isle, one can fidget in the outdoor Jacuzzi, reminisce about the good old days in Bogotá, and, staring past a Calder, a Noguchi, or a Donald Judd, marvel from a safe distance at beautiful Biscayne Bay and all that lies beyond.

This Miami is not so much that of Latin America's deposed tyrants and their flunkies as a biographical register of its hardworking bourgeoisie. When I asked Max Leznik whether he thought that every Latin-American worth more than a million dollars had property in Miami, he replied mirthlessly that, although he couldn't prove it, he suspected that every Latin-American businessman worth a tenth that amount had some small stake in the city. Most of these people have come for the peace and quiet, but even this decision is not without its political dimension. It is, after all, partly the threat of revolution that has driven them north, and the cumulative effect of their arrival has been to buttress the anticommunist consensus of Miami. The city is now the sum of its special interests. Claude Pepper, who once honorably lost his senate seat because he refused to back away from his liberal views on race relations, is, as the oldest congressman in American history, almost exclusively preoccupied with the plight of the elderly. But when he is constrained to pronounce on international politics, it is, as one Miamian put it to me, "to bob up every fifteen minutes to denounce Fidel Castro and every thirty minutes to denounce Yasir Arafat." More interesting even than the act was its ratio. Even a decade ago, the proportions would have been reversed.

In a house on Palm Island, I met a man who had been in the construction business in Lima before, having watched several of his friends pay out every cent they had to rescue their children from kidnappers — whether the perpetrators were Shining Path guerrillas or simply freelancers from the slums of adjacent Callao, no one could say for certain — he sold out and moved his family to South Florida. There was a happy man. As he showed me out to the verandah, we passed a mirror. He paused in front of it for a moment, contemplating his reflection with an unaffected satisfaction I found intensely likable. "I look twenty years younger," he said smiling.

The man took me along to a little Art Deco gazebo ringed with grapefruit and avocado trees. We made small talk while we waited for one of the servants, an impassive Andean peasant straight out of Central Casting (the man barely spoke Spanish, let alone English) to prepare a pitcher of planter's punch. Knowing about my host's concern for his children, I inquired dutifully about the quality of Miami's schools. He didn't want to talk about schools. "Yes, very nice, very nice," he said, cutting me off impatiently. "Do you know what I really like about Miami?" he asked. Question which demands a negative. "Miami is ideal. It's just like Latin America with one marvelous difference." He paused, staring crookedly across at me. Then, bringing his hand suddenly up into a fist, he smashed it down onto the table top as if to pulverize the very idea of what he was about to utter. "No leftists," he said.

*   *   *

It would not, of course, have disturbed my Peruvian friend to hear about all the rightists bombinating around South Florida. Probably, he would have dismissed them. It is certainly true that some of these people have not fared all that well. In Fort Lauderdale, "Winsy" Tabernilla, formerly the head of the Cuban Air Force, has been making a living as a crop duster; his brother, "Silito," once one of Batista's closest aides, ran a military school in West Palm Beach until it closed a few years ago. But among Cuban-Americans, who determine the course of, at the very least, Hispanic politics in South Florida, *La Causa*, the cause, endures. While young, Miami-born Cuban-Americans are hardly enlisting in droves in the secret armies of exile, there remain more than enough recruits for such terrorist groups as Omega 7 and Alpha 66, as well as for more conventional organizations such as the builder Jorge Mas Canosa's Cuban-American National Foundation and its lobbying group, the National Coalition for a Free Cuba, the Cuban National Liberation Front, and the Veterans' Association of Brigade 2506. The men who run these groups, many of whom were at the Bay of Pigs together, not only wield considerable power within the exile community but also in the larger world of South Florida politics, not least in the Republican Party of Dade County, whose revival has largely been due to the efforts of its new Cuban-American activists.

To be sure, this is a far cry from the old days. Right after Castro took power, the CIA, through its Miami station, recruited thousands of Cuban exiles for the sole purpose of overthrowing the regime. In the nineteen-sixties, after the Bay of Pigs fiasco, at least two hundred members of Brigade 2506 received commissions in the United States Army. At least a hundred of these men went almost immediately into the CIA. Over the next ten or twelve years, these anti-Castro soldiers mounted literally hundreds of attacks against Cuba and against Cuban nationals abroad (abroad including, notoriously, the United States itself). Some of these operations were directly sanctioned by the CIA; those that weren't certainly were tolerated by Langley and the Miami station.

The Cuban-American contract employees of the CIA served more or less wherever the agency chose to send them. Felix Rodríguez, for example, whom his friends in Miami like to describe as a "dedicated anticommunist," and whom, more recently, Vice President Bush has called — as if the title had become some kind of Civil Service supergrade — a "patriot," learned his craft in South Vietnam and in the Congo, and, over the past twenty years, has exercised it all over Latin America. With the recent developments in Central America occupying Washington's attention, the Cuban-American networks are again in the news. But it should be remembered that it was from this same world of Miami-based, CIA-linked Cuban-Americans that the Watergate burglars were recruited. The survivors of that "operation" are rather admired in Miami; no one seems to think there is anything particularly wrong with what they did. Today, Eugenio Martínez is a sales manager for a Miami Chevrolet dealer, while Bernard Barker, who returned to Dade County the moment he had completed his term for burglary, became, fittingly enough, a city building inspector.

The professionals have, of course, never gone out of business. Anticommunism is not only their creed, it is their career. But, however invariant their politics, most militant anti-Castro Cubans, including many veterans of Brigade 2506, have become prosperous middle-aged men with businesses to run. Though they grouse about the lack of political fire they see in the younger generation, they themselves have a difficult time these days paying all that much attention to politics. Or at least they did. Today, Cuban Miami is again bemused by the politics of anticommunism. Everyone is talking about Nicaragua.

This is a considerable change. Cuban Miami seemed to be calming down politically by the late nineteen-seventies. For all the pugnacious boasts in the bars of Little Havana or on the Calle Ocho radio stations, attacks against Cuba itself and acts of terrorism abroad appeared to be tapering off. Some veterans were even beginning to admit, in private anyway, that whatever hope there was for unseating communism on the island, it would have to wait until Castro finally died. The relative decline of politics was hardly an unmixed blessing. Not every Cuban turned from infiltrating men into Camaguay to running a legitimate business, like the real estate developer Santiago Álvarez. Others turned their considerable talents for both violence and organization to lucrative illegal pursuits, most particularly, of course, to the marijuana and cocaine trade.

For the late nineteen-seventies were the glory years of the Cuban drug traffickers in Miami. It was the moment when middle-class America fell in love with cocaine and Miami Cubans jumped in to serve as marriage brokers. "Drugs," one ex-dealer recalled wistfully, "were almost legal in those days." In circumstances when, as a veteran of the drug wars put it, dealing in cocaine was "like making your own money, and everyone was so happy you just can't imagine," politics began, slowly but surely, to take a back seat. Drug money has always funded politics, not only in Latin America but throughout the world (today, for example, the Colombian cocaine barons have formed an alliance of convenience with some of the leftist guerrillas). But the pretense among Cubans that the cocaine traffic was a regrettable exigency of war, needed to fund the war against Castro, was scarcely any more convincing than Meyer Lansky explaining from Miami Beach that whatever he had done (and he wasn't, of course, admitting he'd done anything) was in order to defend Israel. Politics was becoming a flag of convenience to conceal big-time drug dealing.

Cocaine was everywhere. A scientist analyzed thousands of twenty-dollar bills in general circulation in Dade County and determined that one note in ten carried traces of cocaine powder. The dealers were not surprised to learn this. Typically, the top note in a wad of money used to pay for a significant amount of cocaine is marked with a number to indicate the total value of that particular stack of bills. One dealer I spoke with recalled with amazement finding that often many of the bills on the insides of these stacks had their own numerical marks, presumably from earlier sales. Dealers don't hoard cash, they try to circulate it as quickly as possible, and it was clear how fast the money was racing through the bowels of the city.

Miami was growing fat on the dealers' leavings. According to the journalist Penny Lernoux, a U.S. Customs spokesman said at the time, "If we were a hundred percent effective, we would so drastically affect the economy that *we* would become the villains." Assiduous enforcement of the drug and banking laws would quite simply have demolished the new international economy of banks and holding companies (not to speak of its attendant real estate market and booming trade in every luxury item from champagne and flowers to limousines and call girls). Public-spirited people might worry about the caustic effects of the drug trade, but, in fact, the city would have been hard pressed to get along without the prosperity that came with it.

As for America, it seemed to have learned nothing from Prohibition. In 1982, with enormous fanfare, Vice-President Bush inaugurated a task force to suppress the importation of drugs into South Florida, and each week, or so it seemed, there would be reports of the "largest ever" shipment ever interdicted (the language of the "War against Drugs" was from the beginning remarkably similar to that used about illegal immigration; all those rocks of cocaine sneaking into the country). The dealers just laughed. "I don't worry," one said to me, "it's just part of the cost of doing business." Another remarked: "They import millions of flowers from Colombia every month into Miami International. No way they're going to be able to check every shipment. Besides, it's a long coastline." And so the drugs get through, seemingly cheaper and of better quality each year. (Even the cocaine one can buy on the spur of the moment — hurriedly but not really furtively — from a hotel parking-lot attendant or a cigarette girl in a disco is usually excellent.)

It is not, of course, in its consumption of cocaine that Miami is remarkable. The drug is everywhere these days. It can be acquired in Midwestern suburban shopping malls and Colorado high school parking lots almost as easily as in the purportedly more effete zip codes of the Atlantic and Pacific seacoasts. However, just as the importance of the automobile for Detroit cannot be measured by the number of cars currently in the possession of the residents of Wayne County and its suburbs, so the feeling is inescapable in Miami that the city is, in reality as well as on "Miami Vice," the corporate headquarters for the cocaine trade in the United States. If the drug were legal, one might even see the sort of civic propaganda that used to be common in American manufacturing centers half a century ago, slogans like "Trenton Makes, The World Takes." For Miami, the possibilities would be endless.

There is, moreover, no reason to think that the traffickers themselves will leave Miami (except, of course, temporarily — fleeing from a bench warrant or an enraged Colombian), even if, as looks possible, the drugs themselves will soon have to be routed through other entry points and the money laundered in Macao or Liechtenstein instead of Coral Gables and Grand Cayman Island. The dealers like Miami; it's home. Seen in this light, a bunch of cocaine cowboys relaxing over their glasses of Roederer crystal at Re-gine's in Coconut Grove comes to seem like nothing so much as a group of weary Ford executives whooping it up in a bar in downtown Detroit before going home to their families in the Bloomfield Hills. Today, drugs are America's genuine growth industry. A few helicopters whirling around in the Florida Strait are no more dangerous to the body of the cocaine business than the mosquitoes they so resemble are to the body of a man taking a walk in the woods.

One does not have to be a Marxist to recognize that there are, in any case, few examples in the history of American cities of any other result, when law and profit have collided, than that of profit winning hand-ily. In a tourist-hungry town like Miami, where the distinction between fame and notoriety has always been sketchy at best, law (as opposed to order) does not rank very high on anyone's list of priorities. And, whatever it has done to people's nerves and morals, cocaine has indisputably been good for a local econ-omy whose tourist business is, in any case, faltering. It is not even clear how upset people were about drugs in Miami, at least until the violence that followed the Mariel boatlift. There was simply too much money going around, and everybody with business to run, from bankers to bartenders, would have been hard pressed not to pay court to these new kings of South Florida, the cocaine cowboys. In Miami, in those days, it was hard to find anyone who believed in much of anything except, perhaps, in the old Texas adage about the golden rule: "The man with the gold makes the rules."

Of course the idyll stopped after Mariel. Cocaine trafficking, which is a fairly orderly business requiring comparatively small numbers of people, is quite un-like the marijuana trade with its crews or "gangs" of men and its deserved reputation for cutthroat double-dealing. There is almost, one comes to feel in Miami, a class barrier between the two businesses. But at the time of the Mariel boatlift, anything in Miami that would float was being used by Cuban-Americans to ferry their relatives north to Key West. To survive this shortage of boats, as well as the increased pressure of the Coast Guard in the Strait, the marijuana dealers had to start dealing cocaine, something they were temperamentally unsuited for. All hell broke loose. "They didn't understand the rules," one former cocaine dealer told me, livid, even today, at the memory. "Cocaine is run on credit, marijuana is up-front cash, and these damn clowns started to shoot people who couldn't pay their bills right away. There was bound to be trouble because, while you can trust most people with a bale of pot, with an ounce of coke you have to be a lot more careful. When the new guys would party away the stuff, they were really partying away their profit; they'd have to add too much cut. That's how the business got so screwed up." Even today, cocaine dealers talk about marijuana sellers much the way cattle ranchers in the American West used to talk about sheepherders.

But Mariel and the intrusion into the cocaine of other, non-Cuban Hispanics also changed the cocaine trade. The criminals whom Castro chucked out along with the refugees were willing to do anything — run drugs, kill people, steal a car, burn down a house — and to do it for absolute rock-bottom wages. Everything, including life itself, became too cheap. The established dealers, who were mostly rather comfortable, middle-class Cuban-Americans, began by using the *marielitos* and soon discovered everything was wildly out of control. The dealers had their families in Miami. Because of this, they had an interest in keeping things orderly. When there were disputes, it was understood that families were off-limits for reprisals. But to the Colombians waiting in the wings, such scruples were not compelling. Leaving aside the widely accepted view that Colombians are the fiercest people in the Americas (a special "profile" on the Colombian community in South Florida which ran in *El Herald* was called, without irony, "The Good Colombians"), the Colombians had no particular interest in playing by the rules. Their families, and, by extension, their morals, were back in Bogotá or Medellín. Where a Cuban coke dealer wanted to be able to live in Miami, Colombians, when they were arrested, would blithely post the astronomical, seven-figure bail and then promptly get on the next plane home. And, terrifyingly, when they thought they had been double-crossed or cheated, they did not just go after the offender but tended to kill his whole family as well.

A French writer once observed, "Behind every fortune lies a great crime." Crime has always been the crooked backstair of upward mobility for new immigrants to the United States. In this, the Miami Cubans are not so very different from the Jews and Italians of sixty years ago. Indeed, despite what is commonly said about Miami, what makes the city unique is not its crime, no matter how awful and degrading, but rather its politics. After all, Miami has in its short civic history already hosted several ethnic varieties of big-time criminals. The Cubans seem to have replaced the Jews and the Italians; perhaps the Colombians will replace the Cubans, if they are not doing so already. Given their phenomenal gift for legitimate business, it is fairly safe to assume that Cuban-Americans will eventually largely eschew crime just as Jewish-Americans did before them. And until recently, it also seemed safe to predict that Cuban Miami was slowly cooling off politically. Now, this no longer seems certain. With each trip I made to Miami, the political temperature seemed to rise. More and more it was impossible, in Little Havana, to get away from the subject of Nicaragua.

Since the fall of the Somoza regime, Miami has become the political headquarters of the Nicaraguan *contras*. This was natural enough, since, as the Sandinist newspaper *Barricada* pointed out accurately in a devastating eight-part series of articles it ran on the city late in 1985, Miami had long been "the rear base of the Latin-American counter-revolution." And proud of it. Where else in the Americas could the *contras* have installed themselves as comfortably? The city was in the United States but it was also familiar, a piece of Latin America. As Arturo Cruz, formerly the Sandinist ambassador to Washington, put it to a reporter from the *Miami Herald*, "Miami is domestic turf for us. It's a little piece of Nicaragua." All the contending elements within the *contras* have their representatives in Miami, and, though San José, Costa Rica, remains the official headquarters of the UNO (the *contra* political organization), everyone knows that most decisions are made in meetings held in Miami. Even the military leaders of the movement have parked their families in Southwest Dade.

Today, Dade County is honeycombed with *contra* offices, information centers, and recruitment and supply facilities. The materiel procured is usually collected in Miami before being shipped to the *contra* base camps in Costa Rica and Honduras. The hundred thousand Nicaraguans who live in South Florida include, at any given time, a few hundred *contra* wounded. They lie in Mercy and Jackson Memorial hospitals, treated, more often than not, by Cuban-American doctors who demand little or no fee. Meanwhile, the *contras* have become the new heroes of Cuban Miami, the frontline fighters against communism. There is a certain perplexing vicariousness about all this adulation. Sometimes, it is hard to resist the idea that the *contras* have become to anticommunism, even in Cuban Miami, what the illegal aliens have become to the American economy.

Not that Cuban Miami is simply applauding from the sidelines, or, for that matter, simply writing out checks. For most Cuban-Americans, Nicaragua is nothing less than a rerun of 1959 in Havana; only this time they think they can win. Scratch a *contra* operation and, somewhere or other, there is a Cuban-American involved. On a governmental level, it seems clear that the CIA has reactivated (if they were ever shut down) the same Cuban-American exile networks it mobilized first for the Bay of Pigs invasion, and, throughout the nineteen-sixties and early seventies, for the secret war against the Castro regime it carried out across the hemisphere. The Cuban-American agents whom the press has already firmly identified reads like a *Who's Who* of the veterans of Brigade 2506. One of them, Felix Rodríguez, was, as "Max Gómez," running the resupply operations to the *contras* from the Ilopango airbase in El Salvador. Such men like to think of themselves as professional anticommunists; were they on the left, most people would call them professional terrorists.

But Cuban Miami is remarkably soft on terrorism, at least the home-grown variety. People tell you that such acts are regrettable but understandable expressions of frustration (a view they would not, presumably, subscribe to were it to emanate from, say, the Shi'ites of Beirut). And they like to evade the question by pointing to such relatively benign spontaneous acts as when, in 1981, a certain Aquilino Carrodeguas, a catering-truck driver at Miami International, decided that, rather than deliver his load of dinners to a waiting British Airways jet, it would be nobler to ram the

Havana-bound Cubana de Aviación plane just down the tarmac. "Long live a free Cuba!" he shouted, as he smashed into the nose of the Castroite airliner.

Carrodeguas received a sentence of five hundred hours community service and the gratitude of all of Cuban Miami. But most blows at the Castro regime were scarcely so defensible. There was, for example, Rolando Otero, a Bay of Pigs veteran and accused marijuana dealer, who, in 1975, set off a bomb at Miami International Airport. Later, in Costa Rica, he tried to assassinate the nephew of the murdered Chilean president Salvador Allende. Interviewed in an American prison, Otero insisted that he regretted nothing. "Political prisoners," he said, "first are defined by their motivation, not their crime." Otero is not an anomaly. In 1976, Orlando Bosch, a Miami pediatrician, and Ricardo "Monkey" Morales, a cocaine dealer and gunrunner, organized the blowing up of the regular weekly Cubana flight from Caracas to Havana. All seventy-three people aboard died, including the Cuban national fencing team. Bosch is certainly as much of a hero in Cuban Miami as the Shi'ite hijackers are in the slums of Beirut. Decent people in both places are doubtless appalled, but most have a favorable gut feeling. In 1983, when Bosch went on a hunger strike in his Venezuelan jail cell, the Miami City Commission proclaimed March 25 "Orlando Bosch Day."

Even moderate figures in Cuban Miami often defend the terrorists. In 1983, Eduardo Arocena, the leader of Omega 7, was arrested in connection with a plot to murder the Cuban ambassador to the United Nations, and afterward Xavier Suárez, who is now the mayor of Miami, remarked that he preferred to think of Arocena as a freedom fighter, not as a terrorist. To

be sure, the number of actual Cuban-American terrorists is small. But then, the number of actual terrorists in any movement is always a tiny fraction.
What is important is that a huge number of Miamians
seem willing to identify themselves as supporting terrorism directed against communists. A poll taken by
the *Miami Herald* in 1983 showed that twenty-two
percent of Miami Cubans believed that anti-Castro
groups were justified in using violence inside the
borders of the United States. Presumably, although
the question was not asked, still more would have
approved of terrorist acts committed outside the
country.

Today, however, the real passions of Cuban Miami
seem focused not on the activities of "freelance" terrorists, or even on those of groups like Alpha 66 or
Omega 7. There is genuine mass enthusiasm for the
Nicaraguan *contras*. Implicit, of course, is the recognition that the exiles' struggle against Castro himself has failed, and that the task is to prevent Castro
from spreading the revolution to the rest of the hemisphere. On the radio stations of the Calle Ocho, there
are incessant appeals for blood donations, reminders
about the *contras'* heroic struggles, fund-raisers. In
the last three years, Cuban Miami has raised millions
of dollars for the cause. And although, as usual, Bay
of Pigs veterans have led the campaign, they were
already preaching to the converted.

There are said to be a few dozen Cuban-Americans
fighting with the *contras*. They are unlikely to make
a great deal of difference. What has made a difference
is the support of the Cuban-American community as
a whole. Cuban-American doctors regularly travel down
to the *contra* base camps along the Honduran-Nica-

raguan border to perform operations on *contra* wounded. Recently, they were accompanied by a famous Cuban comedian, Guillermo Álvarez Guedes, who did his bit by entertaining the troops. It is no accident that when it was discovered that the United States had been illegally funding arms shipments to the *contras* with money from its arms sales to Iran, Patrick Buchanan, the White House communications director, chose to defend the policy in Miami. Before a wildly cheering, largely Cuban-American crowd, Buchanan excoriated the press. The crowd shouted back, "Traitors," and held up signs which read, "Nicaragua is the issue, not Iran."

In reality, the issue was not Nicaragua but Cuba. As Dr. Manuel Alzugaray, the Miami orthopedic surgeon who has been largely responsible for organizing Cuban-American medical aid to the *contras* and who himself has made twenty-nine trips to the Honduran border, put it: "If you do something against Nicaragua, it is going to be bad for Castro because he is helping them. Castro is the cancer. You have to hit him." Phil Rodríguez, a plastic surgeon who has treated many wounded *contras* at his own expense, probably summed up the feelings of many Cuban-Americans when he said: "I wasn't able to do anything to change things in Cuba."

In a sense, what Rodríguez and many like him mean is that by involving themselves in Nicaragua they are refusing to abandon the idea of the Cuba they left and to which, in all likelihood, they will never return. Curiously, it was a *marielito* I met late one night in a coffee shop on the Dixie Highway who put this in perspective. I had spent the evening with a group of Cuban-Americans in long and useless argument about the *contras*. It had been one of those conversations in which everyone is speaking from absolutely fixed positions and what goes on is less a discussion than a series of predictable recitals. The *marielito* asked me what I thought of *Scarface*. Relieved to be talking about something else, I quoted to him Guillermo Cabrera Infante's line that "those who forget the movies of the past are condemned to see remakes," but then I realized he wouldn't know the original with Paul Muni. The thought of there having been an earlier version seemed to amuse him intensely. "It's about Italians and liquor?" he kept repeating.

After a while, I asked him what he thought of Cuban-Americans. He thought for a bit and said: "Those who came before us still think that they will find a way to go back. To do it they would have to travel through time, not just get in a boat. There is no pre-Castro Cuba anymore. Cuba is his, just as Fidel says." Then, grinning at me under the harsh neon of the diner, he remarked, "But perhaps Miami is ours, don't you think?"

ON THE EVE of one of the last visits I made
to Miami before sitting down to write, I was invited
to a dinner given by a well-known New York collector
of primitive art. Along the dining room walls stood
elaborate, intricately illuminated displays of Inca,
Nazca, and Toltec pottery. It was, I think, no mere
trick of light that caused me to see the faces depicted
on these artifacts as nearly exact images of the Indian
servants who, at the moment, were gliding amongst
us with the fish course. Although no one at the table
appeared to be Latin-American or Spanish, many, as
they served themselves, murmured a Spanish *"gracias"* in place of an English "thank you." The servants
themselves paid no notice, as they moved noiselessly
between the table and the kitchen. My dinner companions were an American model and her Belgian eth-
nologist boyfriend. It was from him, toward the end
of the meal, that I heard the story of the illegible pots.

It seemed that, for quite a long time, classical ar-
chaeologists had been at a loss to account for a particular type of Attic pottery, which, while conforming
in most other respects to the inscribed, pictorial vases

and amphoras common to the Ancient World, bore inscriptions in an unknown language. Over the years, a number of ingenious attempts had been made to decipher these inscriptions, but, as it turned out, the solution was far simpler. For in the end everyone agreed that the lettering was nothing more mysterious than plain gibberish. Unable to write themselves (or, presumably, even to hire people who could), these artisans had nonetheless been astute enough to recognize that their pots, no matter how finely made, would be incomplete without the adornment of some sort of lettering. The nonsense writing was the best these potters could do. Earlier in the evening, I had told the Belgian and his discreetly yawning friend about my visits to Miami. Whatever the political acumen of classicists, experts in Peruvian ceramics tend to know a lot about politics in Latin America. I was not surprised when he ended his story about the Greek potters by speculating that, had they lived today, they would probably be waiting for some boat in the Bahamas that would ferry them across to South Florida.

I had intended, during this trip to Miami, simply to tie up a few loose ends. It had been a month or so since I had last flown south, and the plane had barely touched down before I realized once again Miami's immense and troubling power. That visit, the city seemed all rain and regret. I sought out the company of the new immigrants, and even in conversations with the most prosperous of them, it struck me continually how aching was their nostalgia for the places they came from. If they were relieved to be safely in Miami, then the feeling was one of an unhappy, dyspeptic relief. Later, as I sat in my hotel room, listening to the Anglo radio stations disgorge their familiar cargo of xenophobic rancor (leavened, as usual, by the omnivorous frenzy of the ads), I kept wanting to call in myself, to remind these people that even if the direst predictions of the Anglos wind up coming true, and the Hispanics do, indeed, "hijack" Dade County, this act of geographical piracy will, in fact, be an act of despair, a last resort. And if the sounds of Spanish — the new "kitchen" language, literally and figuratively, of the United States — grate on the sensitive Anglo ear, it is only decent to remember what Miami must look and sound like to this legion of befuddled peasants who spend their days cleaning up after the people they uniformly refer to as "the Americans." In the *Miami Herald* the following morning, there was a story about geologists having decided that the Americas were closer together millions of years ago. I doubted it.

One can almost hear the noise it makes as Miami, that great, tempting orifice, sucks the immigrants north. But though this is not a new American story, there is now a difference. A century ago, the implacable realities of geography meant that, over time (though, of course, a longer time than people like to recall), most immigrants began to forget the old country in much the way that even the most bereaved of lovers eventually ceases to be able accurately to picture a loved one's face. Now, the simple accessibility of the entire world via air travel makes such a forgetfulness all but unattainable. Paradoxically, it seems the fact that one can arrive anywhere from anywhere else in a matter of a few hours means that no one in fact ever leaves anywhere. Thus in Miami every alien and immigrant cannot but know that the journey home requires nothing more than some cash and a ride to Miami International. It turns out that in Miami, that paradigmatic city of exiles, tourists, and refugees, even the refugees can be tourists as well.

More even than the port of Miami, Miami International Airport has become a heady mixture of Ellis Island and "The Love Boat." At every arrival gate, people seem to be throwing themselves into the arms of waiting relatives. As the tides of Spanish, and, occasionally, of Yiddish, swell and recede, the only participants who seem to be keeping their heads are the inevitable group of chauffeurs who, immune to the general hubbub, wait incuriously for their passengers, who can turn out to be anyone from tennis player to coke dealer to garment manufacturer. Down the concourse, at the check-in counters of airlines like Air Jamaica, Dominicana de Aviación, and Viasa, even waiting takes place noisily, in a welter of electronic gizmos, baby carriages, and, more often than one likes to think, boxes of canned food. The atmosphere among these families waiting to go home on a visit is half-carnival, half-bread riot. Meanwhile, the airport staff, mostly Cuban of course, pays almost no notice. They have seen it all before.

If the arrival is desperate and exuberant, this jauntiness dissipates in the dark. Late in the evening, along Coral Way, the Dixie Highway, or the Tamiami Trail in Southwest Miami, there are always groups of men clustered in Cuban coffee shops, all-night diners, or, when they are feeling flush, in low-rent piano bars where matronly hookers whose coppery skins scarcely match their blonde, beehive hairdos will croon "Guantanamera" or some other ersatz Caribbean tune for the price of a couple of drinks. It is these lonely, underpaid laborers who are the stuff of Anglo Miami's nightmares — the chromosomatic imperialists, as Carlos Fuentes once aptly described them, who are transforming the United States.

Mostly, they talk about money, women, and home. The only difference is that they do so in Spanish. Everywhere in Miami, whether to the backdrop of deserted office plazas, refurbished Art Deco hotels, or along the endless boulevards with their monotonous groupings of auto-body repair shops, diners, K-Marts and Publix markets, gun shops, and cut-rate furniture stores, the immigrants hold on to the images of the places they have come from. "My country is so beautiful," a Costa Rican busboy said to me, apropos of nothing, as I sat at two A.M., closing out some newly glitzed bar on Washington Avenue in South Miami Beach (the place had, typically enough, been a Jewish dairy restaurant in its previous incarnation). Some days later, a Colombian parking-lot attendant explained that he couldn't bring my car right away and to excuse him but, he remarked with a transfiguring smile, "Now I am talking to my country."

To be sure, none of this longing or this sentimental recreation of the ways of "home" made the choice of coming to Miami seem any less unavoidable. "Back home it's hopeless," a Honduran shopkeeper observed to me bitterly. I had had one drink too many, and, perhaps impertinently, I asked him what he thought the solution was — as if I believed in solutions. "I think," he replied only half-mockingly, pointing down to my Japanese tape-recorder nestled soggily among the empty Heineken bottles, "that we need a few Asian dictators." Less gently than I ought to have, I gestured abruptly in the general direction of the bar's proprietor, a massive, red-haired Cuban, and to his cash register, a high-tech job whose elegant lines were disturbed by a red, white, and blue sticker reading, "Viva Reagan." "You have them already," I said.

They also, of course, had the Tower of Babel. At the airport, the "Miami Vice" T-shirts now vied with a line of leisure wear that simply read, "Exotic Miami." During these last trips, it often seemed to me that even the radio signals were getting garbled, tangled up with one another. One Haitian cabdriver I encountered with the incongruous name of François Roosevel (pidgin for FDR, I wondered) flipped impatiently from a Cuban station fervently praising Colonel North and covert aid to the *contras*, past a Country and Western one where Jesus was being asked to do things which were never in His job description, to, at last, the local Haitian broadcast. Predictably, the message was a complaint. "We are misunderstood by the American people," the announcer said. "They do not know that we are mostly good people, that we have a good culture. But Americans misunderstand it." Later, a caller — all this was, of course, taking place in an English that was at best intermittently comprehensible — congratulated the disc jockey for the way he explained Haitians to the Americans. "We are all the way behind you," she assured him. The cab crossed onto LeJeune Road under a moon so full it seemed swollen.

I began going to Miami when the hoopla marking the centennial of the Statue of Liberty was just getting into gear. Within months, every other television ad was pressing viewers for donations for the refurbishment of "The Lady." Immigration was being talked about as if it were a great American tradition, but, also, as if it had ended. Tartly, Tom Bradley, the mayor of Los Angeles, remarked that while no one was arriving at Ellis Island, his city was receiving more immigrants than ever before and that he had half a mind to build a new Statue of Liberty in the L.A. harbor. Miami, which needed no reminding of the contemporaneity of immigration, was scarcely in a mood to undertake such a civic project, even tongue in cheek.

By the halfway point of my trips to South Florida, *Time* magazine had run a cover in which a sea of colored faces — Inca, Han, Bantu, and Dravidian — was portrayed as the constituent parts of America's "New Melting Pot." The newspapers, not least in South Florida, where the story had a special urgency, were chronicling the furious (and largely symbolic) effort at immigration reform then underway in the Congress. Everybody would have preferred to do nothing; immigration was simply too hard. But somehow the bill got passed. As one congressman remarked in the heat of battle, "That bill's like Dracula; you just can't seem to kill it off." Largely, the nation seemed to view Miami as an example of America gone wrong, whether the subject was illegal immigration, cocaine, or bilingualism. In New York, people who thought Miami looked exactly as it was portrayed on "Miami Vice" assured me solemnly that the city was no longer part of America.

Meanwhile the Ellis Island festivities lumbered on. In commemoration of the Statue of Liberty, a New York bank issued special Visa credit cards with the Lady's head on it. Nationwide, the Coca-Cola company began ornamenting its cans with pictures of all the countries that had furnished immigrants to the

United States. Each can had a map of the country in question, the number of people who had come to America from it, and a thumbnail sketch of the place. It was sublime. The writers appeared simultaneously to be trying to say something generous about these "supplier" countries while making it clear that the immigrants had had every reason to want to get out. The countries in question might be as small as Wales or as large as Mexico; somehow this was all the same thing. I started my collection almost immediately, and these empty soda cans began to pile up on my desk.

For Brazil: "Between 1951–1980, 33,100 Brazilians immigrated to the United States. Their homeland, which occupies nearly half the area of South America, is the 5th largest country on earth. Brazil gave the world the Samba, the Bossa Nova, and produces about one-fourth of the world's coffee." For Mexico: "Between 1951–1980, more than 1,399,800 Mexicans immigrated to the United States. Their native country, situated along America's southwestern border, is nearly 35% natural forest. Mexican artisans are well-known for their exceptional weaving, pottery, and silverwork." For Japan: "About 131,000 Japanese immigrated to the United States between 1951–1980. Nearly one-half of the cultivated land on their Pacific island country, none of which is more than 100 miles from the sea, is devoted to rice production." For Korea: "More than 314,800 South Koreans immigrated to the United States between 1951–1980. Their homeland, which has one of the highest population densities on earth, (1018 people per square mile) is one of the world's leading fishing nations, and the location of one of the largest tungsten mines on earth." For Spain: "Traveling from Spain to the United States by 1970 were 225,574 immigrants — 72,636 of them through Ellis Island. Spain is a world leader in the production of cars and ships; it is well-known for its bull-fighters; and from 1900 to 1925, over 80% of the Spanish immigrants were male." I decided, after a great tussle with myself, that my favorite had to be China. "About 331,900 Chinese immigrated to the United States between 1951–1980. Their homeland has the distinction of having used a written language for more than 3000 years and is credited with the invention of fireworks."

By this benign and barbarous accounting, the world was little more than a well-stocked ice-cream store whose flavors made up the American tortoni. Or perhaps, the country was meant to seem like a zoo, a repository of peoples — though what the purpose of the experiment was no one could say for sure. The more credible explanation (no one can really think of themselves as chocolate ripple ice cream or as a rare gazelle) was that this great event called immigration had in the final analysis simply never happened. Or if it had, it had been pureed through that benevolent maw called immigration so it was as *if* it had never happened. All these picturesque people had wound up as . . . Coca-Cola drinkers, perhaps. But in Miami, as in the rest of the real United States (not the one shown on television), people were wondering whether the miraculous apparatus was still in functioning order.

On an early morning flight to Miami, I was reading fitfully when a smooth yellow hand came into view, squeezing me delicately but insistently on the biceps. I looked sharply across the aisle to find a middle-aged Cambodian man staring fixedly back at me. Next to him, a woman of about his own age, and, beyond her, three small girls. They all were wearing identical running shoes on their small feet.

The plane was just beginning to move toward take-off, but though the seatbelt signs were of course on, these people could do little but stare at the unfamiliar buckled objects knocking against the seat cushions in time to the jostlings of the aircraft as it bumped up the runway. From his pocket, the man withdrew a card and handed it across to me. It smelled of the tropics and turned out to be a sort of travel document identifying the bearers as "sponsored refugees," in transit from a camp in eastern Thailand to a resettlement center in Dade County run by the Methodist Church. Apparently the group had been sent south unaccompanied. Certainly I was not surprised that the stewardesses on the flight, their hands as usual more than occupied with all the other ethnic dramas attendant on the Miami run, had somehow neglected to show the Khmer family how the seatbelts actually worked. And why should the refugees themselves have known?

It is an odd experience to try to teach someone to perform an action which you yourself have assimilated so completely that you all but don't any longer know how to demonstrate it to somebody else. For a moment, I felt myself seized by an almost complete apractic panic. Luckily, whether because he understood or because he felt humiliated, I have no idea, the Cambodian smiled at me. Relieved, I smiled back, and, together, we mimed the faintly obscene mechanics of fastening a seatbelt until he seemed sure he'd gotten it right. What seemed to interest him was how to unbuckle the thing. Nodding, the man turned back toward his family and buckled them in. The plane lurched suddenly into the air. A few minutes later, the movie came on. It was a promotional piece about South Florida, all beaches, bikinis, and high-rises. The Khmers watched mesmerized as, around them, babies squealed, teenage girls yammered away in cheerful Spanish, and, at the rear of the aircraft, a group of Hasidic Jews began to pray.

The great travel story of our time is called migration. In the nineteen-sixties, Marshall McLuhan made his celebrated remark that the world was on the way to becoming a global village. In the decades which have followed, the Third World, that not altogether convincing catchphrase for the majority of people on the earth, has indeed borne him out, but in ways he doubtless never anticipated. For the global village in which we actually live is quite different from the one prophesied in the gleaming, somewhat suburban blue-prints of McLuhan or Buckminster Fuller. Those places were going to be free of everything that was unpleasant (death, significantly, is almost never mentioned in such futurological speculation except as a sound example of ecological practice, or, occasionally, as a problem of waste disposal). In retrospect, all the talk about geodesic domes, climate-controlled environments, and subterranean horticulture reminds one of nothing so much as the gaseous prognosticating of the popular science magazines of the nineteen-twenties and nineteen-thirties — a landscape of historical wishful thinking that probably reached its apogee in the kempt promenades of the 1939 New York World's Fair. Recently in Miami, the Mitchell Wolfson Center for Propaganda Arts (significantly, the only really first-rate collection on public view in Dade County is a museum of popular arts) put on a show of memorabilia from world's fairs all the way back to the Crystal Palace in 1851. As I walked through the exhibition with an English friend, he remarked how such optimism about the future would be inconceivable today. "One simply hopes, against most of the evidence, that things won't get too much worse," he said.

A world's fair is a kind of anthology, and, like most anthologies, it has something of an apocalyptic quality. Perhaps the image of Noah's Ark adrift in the Flood simply cannot be expunged. And Miami, of course, is a sort of world's fair. At the 1925 exhibition at Wembley, the visitor could tour "the entire world and its peoples" in one afternoon. Today, the visitor to Miami encounters not just America, as citizens of the United States call their country to the intense annoyance of everyone else in the hemisphere, but the Americas. There is no escaping the global village, after all.

In the slums of Kuala Lumpur and Mexico City, in Caracas, Libreville, and Port-au-Prince, even in Fidel Castro's Cuba, millions tune in every week to watch "Miami Vice." These people may not have enough to eat; they may believe that the twelfth imam of Shi'ism is on his way back to redeem them; nevertheless, it is virtually certain that they also have a passion for Sonny Crockett. In some poorer tyrannies, often the only photographs visible in shops and seedy offices are the obligatory shot of the despot himself and pictures of American television stars. Thus, while Europeans, who for the most part not only live better than Americans think they do but live better than Americans, now don't have any crying need to migrate to the United States, much of the rest of the world feels rather differently. When President Jimmy Carter met with Deng Xiao Ping in 1980, he chided the Chinese premier on the lack of freedom of movement in the People's Republic. Deng responded curtly. "How many," he asked, "do you want to take in? Ten million?"

It is said that the present rate of combined legal and illegal immigration to the United States is about six hundred thousand per year. Overnight downtown Los Angeles went from being overwhelmingly white to constituting the third largest Mexican city in the world, excepting only Guadalajara and Mexico City itself. Ten percent of the population of the Caribbean now can be found in the United States. On the face of it, this would seem to be the great, overwhelming event of late twentieth-century America, and yet, whether out of moral indolence, or, perhaps, because this extraordinary third wave of immigration largely coincided with another great migration — that of the American middle classes to the suburbs — the subject is one which no one wants to think about very much. Still, the change is so vast that there are Americans not yet even thirty whose childhoods, in retrospect, took place in another country. On this subject, at least, more can be learned by looking at a collection of twenty years' worth of the yearbooks of an urban high school than from the American policy debate.

Migration is, of course, an old fear and fascination in America. The visitor to Miami today may now feel what Henry James felt when he returned to the Lower East Side of New York in 1904. In his *The American Scene*, James described a walk he took in the heart of immigrant, Jewish New York:

It was the sense, after all, of a great swarming, a swarming that had begun to thicken, infinitely, as soon as we had crossed to the East side and long before we got to Rutgers Street. There is no swarming like that of Israel when once Israel has got a start, and the scene here bristled, at every step, with the signs and sounds, unmitigable, unmistakable, of a Jewry that had burst all bounds. . . . It was as if we had been thus, in the crowded, hustled roadway, where multiplication, multiplication of everything, was the dominant note, at the bottom of some vast sallow aquarium in which innumerable fish, of overdeveloped proboscis, were to bump together, for ever, amid heaped spoils of the sea.

In the immediate aftermath of the First World War, more effective, if less scrumptious, pieces of prose were written in response to this general fear of the immigrant tide. In the nineteen-twenties, the immigration laws themselves were tightened to exclude immigrants from southern and eastern Europe (Asian immigration had been curbed by the frankly named Chinese Exclusion Act of 1882, while Mexican immigration was already being encouraged or curtailed according to the Southwestern growers' need for stoop labor). This virtual prohibition of new immigrants, which, along with the passage of the Volstead Act banning alcohol in the United States, was a kind of high-water mark for small-town, Protestant America (they lost their third cause, the attempt to ban the teaching of evolutionary theory, in the wake of the Scopes trial of 1925), remained in force for several decades. Even Hitler's rise did not result in any significant relaxation of the statute. After the onset of the Cold War, however, a series of exceptions began to be allowed for the large numbers of political refugees fleeing communist countries in eastern Europe. In the wake of the Hungarian uprising of 1956, over 150,000 Hungarians were admitted to the United States under a special waiver. The Cubans who have come since 1959 have benefited from the same statutory exception. In 1965, the racist provisions of the immigration law were largely repealed. Congressman Emmanuel Cellar, the sponsor of the legislation, assured his colleagues that there would be little or no change in the demographic makeup of the United States.

In fact, of course, the change was staggering. Even those Coca-Cola cans record the story. Immigration from Europe largely ended by 1970 — a fact discreetly conceded by the phrase "By 1970, over blank number of (Italian, German, etc.) immigrants had entered the United States." For the countries of the Third and Fourth worlds, the record of immigration begins in 1951 and is ongoing. It is the sheerest fantasy for many Americans to imagine that, had the Cubans not arrived, Miami would have remained as it was. In reality, as the Miami-based Monsignor Bryan Walsh has observed, the Hispanicization of South Florida was geographically inevitable. In the Caribbean, he wrote, "The surplus population migrates." The difference between Miami and the other cities of the American Sunbelt is not Latins but a particular people — the Cubans. As Walsh has rightly said, without the Cubans Miami would have been a poor, heavily Hispanic city instead of a rich, heavily Hispanic city. This does nothing to dampen what people feel; it only leads them to misidentify their target. Often when people in New York, or Los Angeles, or even Fort Lauderdale or Bal Harbor, would tell me how much they hated the city Miami had become, I would think: "It's the future they hate." And Henry James would have understood perfectly.

It should not be surprising that immigration provokes such intense, unhappy intensities of feeling. Most people are utterly unprepared for this global village they never had the slightest desire to inhabit. For people who don't believe in anything very strongly, the realities of modern life encourage apocalyptic thinking. In truth, there is no reason, just because things seem to be growing worse, that, conveniently, they have to end in some great bang. But who would have imagined, thirty-five years ago, that to give only one, picturesque, example, close to a quarter of the population of West Berlin would be Turkish? Separated only by the Mediterranean, western Europe too has its common border with the Third World. Indeed, a traveler with a yen to recapture the all-white Europe of half a century ago had best nose his way East. For the moment, at least, life in the Soviet Empire is not a fantasy that appeals much to the poor of the world. Marianne Faithfull's hit song of a few years back had things about right: "Say it in broken English." They do.

In western Europe, of course, immigration has always been synonymous with some sort of violent intrusion. Today, for the first time since the Turks swept toward Vienna (now Turks sweep Vienna), significant new additions are being made to the populations of the major European countries. This reverses, in the space of only a couple of decades, a centuries-old movement toward the diminution of difference in appearance, language, and customs everywhere in Europe. It is this about-face that gives such a particular shock value to the sight of the mosque in Regent's Park or of the daily appearance of Arab men at prayer in the streets of Marseilles. Traditionally, after all, people imagined that mass migration went hand-in-hand with conquest — hence that martial imagery, which, along with medical metaphors of plague and metastasis, almost invariably accompany even the most levelheaded of recent discussions about immigration in Europe. In Spain, people in the south talk without irony of an Arab "reconquest"; in France, a Sunday newspaper ran a photo in its color supplement of Marianne, the national symbol, clad in the chador of militant Islam.

In the United States, a country which for a long time seemed to believe that it could somehow be receptive to immigrants and, simultaneously, immune to the historical baggage they brought with them, there is no panic in the European sense concerning the overturning of tradition. In this sense, at least, the new immigration sits easier on Americans than on Europeans. The problem is that Americans never entirely believed they lived in a world. It was over there, at the far edge of the horizon. But now, the hemisphere seems to be coming ashore, everywhere in the United States, but, particularly, in South Florida, that bit of the continent closest to the Caribbean. It has gotten to the point where in Miami a great many Anglos have begun to perceive even the humblest job-seeker from the islands as nothing less than a conqueror in disguise. To Anglo discomfort, contrast Cuban ease. Indeed, Cubans are probably the only people who really do feel comfortable in Dade County these days. Miami is their town now; the only question is what they are going to do with it, and, of course, what it will do to them.

For a long time, I waited for the Coca-Cola cans with Cuba on them to make their way into the stores. Coca-Cola issued Colombia (it was, the can read, "the world's major source of emeralds, enjoys the world's largest platinum deposits, and is the leading producer of mild coffee"), but, hard as I searched, there was no Cuba. I saw it for the first time as I waited on the checkout line at my neighborhood supermarket in New York. The man in front of me, scraggly bearded, in his early thirties, had on a Harvard T-shirt and wore a button that read, "I refuse to grow up." Nestled in the crook of his left arm was a six-pack of Coke bearing the imprint of the celebrated island itself. For Cuba: "Between 1951–1980, more than 611,900 Cubans immigrated to the United States. Their homeland, the largest island in the West Indies, located about 90 miles from Key West, Fla., has more than 30 types of palm trees, and is one of the world's leading producers of sugar."

On my last trip to Miami, I decided, on an impulse, simply to fly on to Key West. There, on Duval Street, in between a sleazy T-shirt store and what looked like a somewhat overambitious restaurant, lay the weathered hulk of a boat which, twenty years before, had carried Cuban refugees across the Florida Strait. The peeling memorial sign saluted "those men, women, and children who risked death for freedom." Sixty years before, Cuban socialist cigar makers had listened to readings of Cervantes, Max Nordau, and Jules Verne, as they worked down by the Mallory Dock. José Martí had spoken often in a meeting hall on Duval in the years before the Cuban War of Independence. The building later became the property, to everyone's considerable embarrassment, of the Castro government, though, today, back safely in the hands of South Florida Cuban-Americans, it is being refurbished as a Cuban "cultural center" by Jorge Mas Canosa's Cuban National Foundation. Late that night, unable to sleep, I walked from my hotel to the Mallory Dock. A solitary cabdriver was leaning against the hood of his old Chevy, puffing on a thick joint. I asked him to point out the direction of Cuba.

I went back up to Miami the next morning. During the flight, the pilot pointed out a reconnaissance balloon hovering in the air over one of the smaller keys. "If you look off to your left," he announced, "you'll be able to see the balloon we pilots call 'Big Bertha.' She sort of keeps an eye on Cuba for us, and she also tries to put the kibosh on those drug smugglers who've been acting up lately." As in the seventeenth and eighteenth centuries, pilot and passengers alike took it absolutely for granted that the Caribbean was a war zone, a smugglers' lake. In a way, the notoriety just made the keys more of a tourist draw. After this, I was not surprised, when the small DC-3 landed with a worrying, geriatric thump at Miami International, to find that the "gimmick" present of the moment, on sale in the airport stores, was a wad of fake money. These wads were displayed in piles inside a thick, rectangular attaché case. On the way in to Coral Gables, the cabdriver began to sing along enthusiastically with a rock song whose lyric repeated, "Too many people [or "peoples," as the driver said it], too much confusion." The film *Top Gun* was playing on the Calle Ocho. We turned down 37th, heading for the Miracle Mile.

That evening, I had dinner with Raúl and Ninón Rodríguez. I had met them on a previous visit, and thought them the most glamorous couple in Cuban Miami. We had a long-standing date to see the slides they had shot during a return visit they had made, extraordinarily enough, to Cuba in 1980. Through the open sliding doors of their house in Southwest Miami (he is an architect, she a teacher at F.I.U.), we could look out onto a garden of cypresses, ficus, and exotic tree ferns, delicately lit for effect. After dinner (she had cooked), he carefully made three cups of the best coffee I have ever tasted. Then the slide show began.

The Rodríguezes were both born in the rich Havana neighborhood of Miramar. Understandably, they had wanted to spend a good deal of their short visit to Cuba exploring the places where they had lived as children. They had, of course, found most of the houses abandoned. "Ten thousand people lived here along Fifth Avenue," Raúl said. When I asked him where these people lived now, I already knew the answer. Smiling, he gestured toward his backyard, an elegant arc of the arm that seemed to take in all of Coral Gables and prosperous Southwest Miami. "They live here, I suppose," Raúl said. In fact, when the Rodríguezes returned from their trip, they presented at least three dozen former residents of Miramar with photographs of their old homes.

The slides confirmed the obvious. What was remarkable about Havana and Miami was not their differences but the ways in which the two cities resembled each other. Miramar looked like an unkempt slummy version of Coral Gables. The same trees grew along the avenue and, indeed, many of the houses themselves turned out to have been built by the same architectural firms and, in any case, were in much the same tropical "Deco" or "Mediterranean" style. The great palaces of the South Florida boom like the Biltmore Hotel in Coral Gables, had, Raúl told me, their counterparts in Havana. The New York firm that had erected the Biltmore in 1926 had, the following year, built the splendid Sevilla Hotel in Havana. If there was a metaphor for what was going on with the Cubans in South Florida, it was neither military nor oncological but rather the historic sameness of a shared botanical environment. As children, the Rodríguezes had come regularly to Miami. It was scarcely a foreign place. It seemed, in context, bizarrely fitting that Mitch Maitique, the new Cuban-American president of F.I.U., had recently bought Addison Mizner's old house in Coral Gables.

Before they drove me back to my hotel, Ninón Rodríguez told me that before she had revisited Cuba, she had been racked by dreams about Havana. Now, she said, she rarely, if ever, had those dreams, though she wanted very much to make another trip. In this, the Rodríguezes are exceptional. In most of Southwest Miami, Cuban-Americans still find themselves stranded in these dreams. They have suffered for it, emotionally though not materially, and so has the city of Miami, that place, that "Magic City," itself founded as a dream. The slide show ended with a shot of Havana's José Martí International Airport seen from the air and then with an image of the plane banking over Key Biscayne. The two views were not easy to tell apart.

It was enough. I did not want to see anyone else in Miami. The following morning though, before leaving, I made one last trip to the botanical garden called the Parrot Jungle. There, in a setting of rare flowers, cypresses, Indian ficus, and tropical palms, hundreds of exotic birds roam and call. By a pool, dozens of pink and orange flamingos, some perched inevitably on one leg, pecked at the surface of the water. By the entry-way, Brazilian tourists — themselves a spectacle — fed seeds to the bright, gaudy macaws and to subtle white and pinkish cockatoos. Sulfur-breasted toucans and emerald toucanets pushed their odd, upsetting beaks against the sides of their cages. I thought I heard a dapper parakeet say hello, and, startled, leaned against a fence. Below, a lazy alligator, its head half-buried in the ooze, swished its tail fractionally.

Although I had probably visited the Parrot Jungle a half-dozen times during my stays in Miami, I had never seen the little show the park put on. This time I sat, rapt, and watched a cheerful, brawny bird-trainer put an assorted menagerie of macaws, cockatoos, and parrots through their paces. One bird could repeat, startlingly, "I love you" and "Here, kitty, kitty, kitty." There was a cockatoo that played poker and another that could slide down a rope with its beak. Two cobalt-blue macaws rolled on command, first left, then right. All the birds had names — slightly old-fashioned American ones like Henry, Tina, and Susie. But though the names might be indigenous, the trainer made much of the fact that most of the birds were not. I noted in my journal that most seemed to come from Latin America.

Of course, the trainer intended only to underscore the exotic character of his act. Still, I doubt I was alone in picking out the other parallels. "One of my macaws," the trainer began, "has received a package from his native country of Colombia." The punch line called for the macaw to open this "package." As it did so, I started to laugh, my mind on other packages Miamians had grown accustomed to receiving from that country. Across the little auditorium, two heavy-set Cuban men who had come with their families stared sharply at me for a moment. Then they too began to laugh.

Toward the end of the performance, a small child asked, "Do the birds ever fly away?"

"Well, they have everything they could possibly want here," the trainer replied, smiling; "just about all they can eat and they even get to choose their own mates." When a cockatoo riding a unicycle across a high-wire made its way past an American flag ("If you focus on the flag when the bird passes, that will give you the best picture," the trainer advised, and several Japanese tourists hastened to obey him), I thought it was time to finally go home.

I left Miami before I reached the airport. It was the first time in all my visits to the city that, though I looked carefully, nothing I saw through the window of the cab seemed to signify very much more than any other short ride through a midsized American city. In the airport, I felt the same abstraction, and it was only when I boarded the plane that, unaccountably, I pressed my face hard against the scored Perspex window. I went on staring down at the city even after the aircraft crossed the first line of clouds. Somehow I imagined I could see Cuba and America — Mom and Dad — watching too, and wondering, as I was, how it would all turn out.